Merciful Meekness

Merciful Meekness

Becoming a Spiritually Integrated Person

Kerry Walters

Paulist Press
New York/Mahwah, N.J.

Scripture extracts are taken from the Revised Standard Version, Copyright ©
1946, 1952, by the Division of Christian Education of the National Council of
the Churches of Christ in the United States of America and reprinted by per-
mission of the publisher.

Cover design by Sharyn Banks
Book design by Lynn Else

Library of Congress Cataloging-in-Publication Data

Walters, Kerry S.
    Merciful meekness : becoming a spiritually integrated person / Kerry Walters.
        p. cm.
    Includes bibliographical references.
    ISBN 0-8091-4119-1 (alk. paper)
    1. Meekness. 2. Mercy. 3. Christian life—Catholic authors. I. Title.
    BV4647.M3W35 2005
    241'.4—dc22

                                                                      2004020833

Published by Paulist Press
997 Macarthur Boulevard
Mahwah, New Jersey 07430

www.paulistpress.com

Printed and bound in the
United States of America

Contents

For Kim Westermann,
who set me thinking on these things

Meekness and Mercy

Many of the problems and sufferings of the spiritual life today are either fictitious or they should not have to be put up with. But because of our mentality we block the total response that is needed for a fully healthy and fruitful spirituality.

Thomas Merton

Public Professions, Private Beliefs

Some books on Christian spirituality are responses to unsympathetic challenges from the outside. Their intended audience is that swelling number of persons who frankly find Christian belief implausible. Other books on the Christian way are addressed to an in-house audience. Their purpose is to challenge complacency or confusion among followers of Christ by nudging them to explore their spiritual tradition more deeply.

I originally conceived this little book as an exercise of the first kind: an insider's response to the secular cynic's charge that the Christian values of meekness and mercy are impractical if not downright harmful in today's hectic and dangerous world. But in the course of writing, as I probed my own thoughts about meekness and mercy and solicited the opinions of friends and colleagues, I began to realize that the outsider criticism I intended to take on is shared to one degree or another by many of us on the inside. Granted, there's a difference in tone and articulation. Outsiders are generally more strident and explicit than insiders. For the most part, doubts about meekness and mercy loudly voiced by non-Christians are either left unspoken or only indirectly hinted at by like-minded Christians. But the skepticism is there nonetheless, and traces of it come through in what we Christians actually *do*, even if it only rarely breaks through in what we say.

In the spiritual life, inconsistency between what we profess and how we wind up behaving in the world is a sign that something's not as it should be. Such inconsistency can usually be explained in one of two ways: Either we're sincere in our beliefs, but fail to follow through on them out of laziness or self-indulgence, or we in fact don't *really* believe what we publicly profess, although we may never have admitted as much to ourselves (and certainly not to others!).

Both of these are serious problems. But the second is far graver than the first. In the first case, chances are good that we're uncomfortably aware of the dissonance between what we say and what we do, and this leaves room for the possibility of turning the corner and making a fresh start. But in the second case, the dissonance is beneath the surface and so typically goes unnoticed or is only dimly and sporadically perceived. It's not garden-variety hypocrisy. Christians suffering from this tension between public profession and private belief aren't pretending to be something they aren't. They're not out to fool others. If there's any deception going on here, it's self-directed. They truly *do* think they believe what they profess. Yet the gulf between utterance and act suggests otherwise.

Let me illustrate this with an example most of us can probably relate to. More than one theologian has noted that, although Christians by definition *profess* a trinitarian God, many of us *act* as if we don't really believe in the trinitarian doctrine at all. During formal worship, we mechanically recite trinitarian formulas and credos and cross ourselves in the name of the Father, Son, and Holy Spirit. But in private devotions and non-liturgical situations, we act like good Unitarians. We have in mind a rather blurry, abstract Creator God who all but sidelines the Son and Holy Spirit. Or we fixate on the incarnate Son at the expense of Father and Holy Spirit. Or, less frequently, we attend for the most part to God as indwelling Spirit and tacitly ignore Father and Son. In all these cases, our acts belie our professed trinitarianism. This needn't mean we're hypocrites, but only that we're confused about what we profess. And we're confused because we misunderstand the Christian concept of who and what God really is.

I believe something similar to this goes on when it comes to meekness and mercy, two spiritual values that everyone, insiders as well as outsiders, acknowledges as mainstays of the Christian way. Let's be honest with one another: We Christians all profess allegiance to meekness and mercy, but we rarely live up to them. Sometimes, as I suggested earlier, the inconsistency is the result of laziness. But just as frequently, it comes from the fact that many of us don't truly believe the pious platitudes we utter. And this is because we insiders are often just as confused about the deep meaning of meekness and mercy as the outsiders who explicitly reject them.

All this gradually dawned on me in the preparation of this book. So what I originally intended as a challenge to nay-saying critics of Christian spirituality evolved over time into a challenge to insiders—myself included—as well. It's no good carping about the splinter in someone else's eye until you've removed the two-by-four from your own.

This book now tries to speak both to those outsiders with a sour taste in their mouths for Christian spirituality, and to insiders like myself who could profit from some clarity about what Christian meekness and mercy *really* mean. I hope my wrestling with the deep significance of these two virtues can help others, Christians and non-Christians alike, come to a better understanding of them.

But I also fear that a few of the things I have to say here may disturb or even anger some readers, especially my fellow believers. If this happens, I beg forgiveness in advance. Yet I can at least claim good precedent. Christ came to shake things up, not hand out canned platitudes. We Christians should follow his example, as best we can, by challenging ourselves to reexamine and rearticulate our basic assumptions with a fervor that outstrips even the hottest criticisms from the outside. Otherwise, we risk becoming whited condominiums.

The Problem

The spark that ignited this exploration of meekness and mercy was a conversation with one of my students, an intelligent, sensitive, and likeable young woman. Like so many college students who suddenly find themselves in a bewilderingly heady snowstorm of new ideas, Kim had fallen into a crisis of faith.

She'd been raised in a conventionally religious household and matter-of-factly accepted what she was handed in Sunday School and church without reflecting very deeply about it. A few courses in sociology, history, and psychology had already started to whittle away at the beliefs she'd always simply taken for granted. But then Kim stumbled across the writings of the nineteenth-century philosopher Friedrich Nietzsche, that brilliant and tormented singer of God's death. His savage vivisection of the Christian values of meekness and mercy utterly shook her foundations. This is what brought her to my office.

Nietzsche's repudiation of meekness and mercy was the immediate cause of Kim's distress as well as my reflections in these pages. But this book isn't about Nietzsche so much as the secular suspicion of Christian spirituality he legitimized. In a very real way, we dwell in a cultural climate whose core values and beliefs are Nietzschean. As we'll explore in some depth later, his influence has trickled down even to those who have never read any of his books, and perhaps don't even know his name.

So in taking on his criticisms of meekness and mercy here, I'm not merely indulging in a bookish philosophical exercise. Rather, I'm responding to the spirit of an age—what might almost be called the "Nietzschean ethos"—that he systematically defined a century and a half ago. Nietzsche was the first and still most articulate prophet of this age. Consequently, if we wish to get clear about the milieu in which we dwell, we must turn to his words. In wrestling with them, we do more than just argue with a long-dead German philosopher. Much more importantly, we confront the deep-seated impatience with Christian spirituality he inspired, an impatience so pervasive in our culture that even self-proclaimed Christians have been marked by it to one degree or another.

Make no mistake: the stakes in this game are high, going far beyond the historical man Friedrich Nietzsche. They involve nothing less than the very possibility of Christian spirituality in the new millennium. To my student Kim's credit, she realized this when she first encountered Nietzsche's assault on meekness and mercy.

The gist of Nietzsche's rejection of Christian meekness and mercy can be easily stated, although responding to it isn't quite so simple. He attacks on two different but converging fronts. In the first place, he argues that meekness and mercy, far from being genuine virtues, in fact are morally repugnant. As if this isn't damaging enough, he goes on to claim that meekness and mercy are irremediably incompatible: one can be meek *or* merciful, but not both. Either way, anyone who takes seriously the Sermon on the Mount's teaching that meekness (the third Beatitude) and mercy (the fifth Beatitude) are blessings is pathetically misguided.

Meekness and mercy are morally repugnant, argues Nietzsche, because they're not what they appear to be. Scripture tells us that both are spiritual gifts that enable us to lead holy lives and grow into the persons God intends us to be. But this is false. Meekness and mercy are actually vices masquerading as virtues— and, like all vices, they're in the insidious business of stunting and distorting their practitioners.

On this reading, what passes itself off as the virtue of meekness—a spirit of humble gentleness that turns the other cheek, refuses to assert self-interest at the expense of others, and eschews violence in thought, word, and deed—in fact is a duplicitous attempt to make timidity and spineless indecisiveness respectable. No healthy person could possibility tolerate the slavishly demeaning attitude of meekness. Only someone hopelessly burdened with a crushing sense of inferiority would be desperate enough to "legitimize" his own brokenness by embracing it as a virtue. Yet Nietzsche thinks this is precisely what Christians do, and concludes that the move shows up Christianity for what it really is: a religion by and for neurotic misfits.

Mercy fares no better at Nietzsche's hands. Christians see it as a virtuous self-giving in which the merciful person, acting out of a spirit of compassionate benevolence, goes out of his or her way to help those who suffer. As Matthew famously says (25:35–45), mercy means feeding the hungry, succoring the ill, clothing the naked, and so on, even when such behavior calls for great sacrifice on the part of the mercy-giver. But as in the case of meekness, says Nietzsche, this is all a smokescreen for what's actually going on. The real motive behind mercy is domination and manipulation. We act "mercifully" because it makes us feel superior to the objects of our mercy. We're strong, they're weak, and in extending aid to them we smugly congratulate ourselves on taking the moral high ground—and, as a bonus, putting the recipients of our "mercy" in our debt. Mercy is thus the primary ploy by which weak and ineffectual persons try to assert control over others. It comes as no surprise to Nietzsche that a religion perversely built on neurotic meekness also preaches the equally neurotic power-play of mercy.

So much for the morally repugnant nature of meekness and mercy. Both are really strategies of dissimulation and manipulation. This is the dirty little secret Christians try to scrub clean with pious platitudes and self-righteous rhetoric.

Nietzsche obviously thinks all this ought to be enough to convince any person of reason and honesty to walk away from the whole business. But Christians, desperate like all neurotics to hang onto their delusions, are remarkably resistant to honest self-examination. So Nietzsche launches an attack from his second front. Even if you reject my claim that meekness and mercy are morally repugnant, he says to Christians, your own definitions of them show them up as contradictory and hence mutually exclusive.

The virtue of meekness (as Christians deceptively preach it, not as it "really" is) invites people to practice humility and lowliness in the face of mockery, persecution, and violence; to renounce self-will, turn the other cheek, and love their enemies. They're obliged to cultivate indifference to the worldly cares and concerns of Caesar's domain, focusing instead on an inner stillness and composure that no external storm can so much as ruffle. Meekness, in short, calls Christians to a life of radical detachment from the world.

So far so good. But the glitch in the machine is mercy (again, as Christians duplicitously preach it, not as it "really" is). At the same time that meekness prescribes passive withdrawal from worldly bustling, mercy obliges a person to actively throw him- or herself into the world to minister to victims of persecution and oppression, and to champion the rights of the hungry, the thirsty, the naked, the ill, the marginalized. This means that the merciful person must not only perform individual acts of charity, but also, when circumstances call for it, take to the streets to denounce perpetrators of injustice. If Christ's example is followed, mercy at times must even be unabashedly partisan in its defense of the downtrodden, routing their oppressors as Jesus chased the money changers from the temple. Mercy, in other words, calls Christians to a life of active engagement in the world.

When expressed in these terms, the incompatibility Nietzsche wishes to demonstrate seems disconcertingly obvious, doesn't it? Christ doesn't say "Be meek *or* merciful," but "Be meek *and* merciful." Yet how can one be both? The first demands gentle resignation, the second zealous resistance. Meekness prescribes humility and silent endurance, mercy righteous anger and noisy advocacy. On the Christian's own terms, then, the spirituality he or she defends is shot through and through with a seemingly irreconcilable contradiction.

Nietzsche's double-whammied challenge was the rock on which my student Kim's faith had foundered. In the first place, she was strongly committed to the Christian call to meekness and mercy. But she was psychologically astute enough to recognize the possibility that meekness and mercy could indeed be self-serving legitimations of temperamental timidity and sly manipulation. She, like most of us at one time or another, had seen self-proclaimed Christians justify quite shameful shenanigans by invoking these two virtues, and honesty obliged her to question her own motives as well. How could she be certain that her embrace of meekness and mercy wasn't a symptom of the neurotic hypocrisy diagnosed by Nietzsche?

In the second place, Kim was deeply committed to the Christian teaching that a humble renunciation of self-will and madcap ambition indeed is essential if one wishes to serve God. At the same time, her anguish at the palpable suffering she perceived in an unjust and frequently cruel world profoundly persuaded her that she was conscience-bound to protest quite unmeekly against it—and that this, too, was a necessary step in the service of God. But the logic of Nietzsche's argument forced her to concede that these two convictions pulled in opposite directions. She saw no way to reconcile them. Meekness provided a way for cultivating silent receptivity to God, but the cost was patiently awaiting a future pie-in-the-sky resolution of present ills. Mercy allowed for a resolute, roll-up-the-sleeves-and-get-to-work activism, but at the frightening expense of losing one's spiritual bearings amid worldly hustle and bustle.

Nietzsche had done his work well. By the time she came to see me, Kim was ready to jump ship.

The Options

I'd like to insist on one point before we go any further: Both Nietzsche's challenge and Kim's distress must be taken seriously by anyone genuinely committed to the Christian spiritual way. It just won't do to dismiss Nietzsche as a splenetic iconoclast who peevishly twists Christian teachings to suit his own purposes. As we'll see in later chapters, he backs up his claims with clarity and rigor. Whatever his private motives, the argument he presents must be examined on its own merits. We can't pooh-pooh Nietzsche's challenge simply by insisting that he's got a personal ax to grind against Christianity.

Similarly, it's callous and condescending to trivialize Kim's distress by writing it off as the growing pains of an intellectually impressionable youngster. Kim had a keen mind, and she'd thought long and hard about Nietzsche's criticisms, turning them this way and that in the hope of discovering some way out. The painful crisis in which she landed was genuine. It deserves to be taken seriously, not patronizingly chalked up to a postadolescent rite of passage.

We must take both Nietzsche's challenge and Kim's crisis seriously for at least three other reasons, ones I've already suggested and will explore in some detail in the chapters that follow. In the first place, many of us privately endorse, to one degree or another, Nietzsche's charge that meekness is merely whitewashed timidity and cowardice. This private contempt for meekness went public in the wake of the terrorist attacks on the World Trade Center and the Pentagon. Pacifist organizations such as Pax Christi and the Fellowship of Reconciliation that called for a nonmilitary way of bringing the perpetrators to justice were branded as cowards. It made no difference that these organizations justified their nonviolent position by appealing to Christ's words in the Sermon on the Mount. In the heat of the moment, many Christians who in other contexts would publicly endorse Christian peace-making let slip their real attitude toward meekness.

Second, many of our actions, whether or not we're aware of the fact, sadly illustrate Nietzsche's claim that mercy is an insidiously disguised strategy for manipulating others. Too often we expect something in return from those on whom we "generously" bestow mercy. At the very least, we demand their gratitude.

Finally, all of us, surely, have been bothered by the apparent tension in Christianity's twin endorsement of gentle meekness and active mercy. How could we not? The dissonance is traceable, as Nietzsche correctly observed, to the scriptures themselves, and the two-thousand-year history of Christian spirituality is to some degree an attempt to come to grips with it. Occasionally the pendulum of opinion swings toward an emphasis of meekness; at other times it careens in the opposite direction toward mercy. Periods that emphasize solitary soul-searching in the desert counterpoint with ones that cry for militant crusading in the name of the "social gospel." What can be said of historical periods can also be said of individuals: Each of us, like my student Kim, is dizzied to one degree or another by the back-and-forth tussle between the call for meekness and the call for mercy. Both speak to our deepest spiritual intuitions, yet feel distressingly at odds with one another.

So: what are our options?

One, of course, is simply to ignore Nietzsche. We can recoil in hyperdefensive denial of his charge that meekness and mercy are morally repugnant subterfuges, and piously insist that the apparent incompatibility between the duties of meek detachment and merciful engagement is just one of those "mysteries" of faith that defy reason.

But this nonresponse won't do. Hiding one's head in the sand won't make the problem disappear. To dismiss out of hand the charge of moral repugnance is to ignore in a psychologically naive way the incredible complexity, particularly when it comes to religious beliefs, of human motives and dispositions. Moreover, to sidestep Nietzsche's claim of incompatibility between meekness and mercy by relegating the tension to the murky black box of "mystery" solves nothing. If anything, it only exacerbates the fragmentation that begins to set in when deep-seated spiritual intuitions that appear to clash with one another are allowed to remain unreconciled. So we ought to be especially cautious about assigning spiritual perplexities the status of "mystery." This isn't to deny either the presence or importance of mystery in the Christian tradition, but only to remind ourselves that easy appeals to it may be justifications for laziness or dogmatism. Intellectual and moral honesty require that we play the mystery card only after earnest attempts at rational reconciliation have collapsed. Doing less trivializes both reason and mystery.

Another option is to bow to Nietzsche's logic and concede check and checkmate. We can grant him his first point, and confess that the Sermon on the Mount's call to meekness and mercy is actually a smokescreen for wily self-service, or we can grant him his second point by acknowledging that meekness and mercy are irreconcilably contradictory.

But this option is not only premature at this point; it's also unthinkable. Granting Nietzsche his first point gives the lie to two millennia of Christian spirituality, and paints Jesus as well as generations of saints as self-deceived neurotics or manipulative scoundrels. Seriously as I think we ought to take Nietzsche's challenge, Christians simply must draw the line at this kind of carnage. For the Christian story is *our* story, the compass by which we orient ourselves in the world. To jettison it is to set ourselves adrift in a universe with no clear horizons or harbors. Saying this obviously doesn't excuse clinging so blindly to every jot and title of our faith tradition that we refuse to retake our bearings when we run into stormy weather. But it does mean that any change of course we make remains solidly *within* the context of the Christian story. The goal is to keep our vessel seaworthy, not scuttle it.

If we grant Nietzsche his second claim, that meekness and mercy are inherently contradictory, we're left with a couple of alternatives that are equally unpalatable. The first, once again, is simply to turn one's back on Christianity as an ill-conceived mishmash of irreconcilable claims. But as we've just seen, this alternative is too destructive to contemplate. It exonerates Jesus and the saints from charges of self-deception and manipulativeness, but no less damningly paints them as hopelessly muddled.

The second alternative is to salvage what we can by rejecting *either* meekness *or* mercy, insisting that the "true" message of Christ is one of total passivity *or* total engagement, and concluding that the contradiction Nietzsche points out is the consequence of garbled tradition. But this is likewise unacceptable. It ignores Christ's clear instruction to cultivate *both* meekness and mercy, and it, too, violates our deep intuitions that each is equally necessary for a balanced spiritual life. Karl Rahner once wisely said that the ultimate goal of Christian spirituality is to enable us to become full-fledged persons.[1] But personhood suggests that those core beliefs and values which comprise our center of gravity form a coherent and cohesive whole, and that outward comportment is compatible with interior conviction. A genuine person possesses what the medievals called *integritas:* a stable but creatively adaptable harmonization of beliefs and motivations, intuitions and concepts, intentions and actions. Our status as persons is diminished when this harmony starts to disintegrate. Instead of leading holistic, well-integrated lives, we lopsidedly veer off in one fragmented direction or another.

To respond to Nietzsche's challenge by downplaying meekness for the sake of mercy, or mercy for the sake of meekness, is to rupture *integritas* and thus damage our spiritual development. Later, we'll explore in some detail why this is. For now it's enough simply to reflect on our own experiences or to examine (without condemning) the lives of Christians whom we suspect suffer from fragmentation.

Most of us have either first or secondhand acquaintance with what happens when meekness and mercy split into opposing camps. Those of us who choose meekness as Christianity's primary spiritual value run the danger of turning a blind eye to our suffering brothers and sisters who cry out for and deserve our compassionate aid. In our zeal for cultivating the "inner" virtues of humility and detachment, we risk becoming self-absorbed narcissists who selfishly put our desire for personal salvation ahead of charity to our neighbors. Those of us who opt for mercy, on the other hand, hazard the danger of becoming professional "do-gooders" so dispersed in a frenetic flurry of "benevolent" busyness that we lose touch with that stillpoint within the soul that properly grounds compassionate action in the world. Either way, *integritas* is fragmented, leading to despair in the first case, burnout in the second, and self-deception in both.

Happily, there's a third way of responding to Nietzsche's challenge that avoids all this: taking Christ at his word and embracing both meekness *and* mercy as necessarily intertwined virtues of the spiritual life. But this option demands that we do some painful self-examination as well as hard thinking about what meekness and mercy actually mean, and how they relate to one another in practical, concrete terms. It requires that we take Nietzsche's challenge seriously enough to understand the grounds on which it's based; to plumb scripture and Christian tradition deeply in order to discern what Jesus intended by the third and fifth Beatitudes; and to courageously resist the temptation to fall back on pious treacle that offers immediate comfort, but actually says little if anything.

Above all, choosing this third option demands that we go into the investigation with the trust that although God is mysterious, he's not a trickster who bamboozles us into seeing black as white, or asks things of us we're incapable of giving. If Jesus told us that spiritual growth requires meekness as well as mercy, we must take him at his word. The fact that our most profound spiritual intuitions also point in this direction clinches the matter. Granted, our personal weaknesses may at times lead us into selfish attitudes and actions we try to dress in the garb of meekness and mercy. But knowing that this is a possibility provides some safeguard against it. Moreover, our individual temperaments quite likely may predispose us to one of the virtues more than the other. Some of us are more naturally inclined to meekness, others to mercy. But the ideal is a creative synthesis of the two that encourages that "total response," as Merton says in the epigraph to this Introduction, "needed for a fully healthy and fruitful spirituality." At the end of the day, God won't judge us on whether we actually *attained* this total response, but on how earnestly we *sought* it. As one fourteenth-century mystic put it, "the path to heaven is measured by desire and not by miles."[2]

This book is an exploration and defense of the third option. It is, if you will, what I wish I'd had the wits to tell my friend and student Kim when she came to me seeking counsel. Chapters 1 and 2 focus, respectively, on meekness and mercy by examining and responding to the Nietzschean rejection of them as morally repugnant. Chapter 3 builds upon the first two by arguing that meekness and mercy, when properly understood, are not only compatible but so essentially complementary that we ought to refer to them in a single breath as "merciful meekness."

As I said earlier, my original intention in writing this book was merely to challenge Nietzsche's criticism of Christianity. In the process, however, I also wound up challenging many of my old ways of thinking about meekness and mercy, dropping some notions, refining others, stumbling across still others. I discovered that many of the "problems and sufferings" (to invoke Merton's words again) through which we Christians struggle in our attempts to understand and live merciful meekness are self-imposed fictions that simply don't "have to be put up with." The upshot, I trust, is that I have a better grasp now than I once did of what it means to be a person walking the path of Christian spirituality, and that there's less dissonance and more *integritas* between my public professions and my private beliefs. My hope is that this book in some small way can also challenge you to reexamine your own journey toward *integritas* and reaffirm your commitment to God in the midst of a dangerously seductive Nietzschean ethos that tempts us away from the blessings of meekness and mercy.

CHAPTER ONE

Meekness

What need was there for the Lord of Majesty to empty himself, to humiliate himself, to make himself little, unless it be that you might do the same? He already proclaims by his example what he will later preach in word: "Learn from me, for I am gentle and humble in heart."...Do not allow such a valuable example to have been given to you in vain; but rather, conform yourselves to this model and be renewed even to the intimate depths of your being.

Bernard of Clairvaux

"Meek as a ———"

In a bygone era innocent of radio and television, parlor games were popular ways of passing time. One such game, described by Charles Dickens in *A Christmas Carol*, seems to have been a special favorite. It was a guessing game that tested one's familiarity with conventional similes. Players were given the first part of a simile, such as "tight as a ———" or "pretty as a ———," and in quick order had to come up with the appropriate ending: "drum" or "peacock." The fun of the game was to keep the similes flying at such a fast and furious pace that players became confused and tongue-tied.

If we played the game today, it's just conceivable we might run across someone unaware that a drum's made from membrane stretched tightly across a rim, or has never thought of peacocks as particularly lovely creatures. But it's difficult to imagine that anyone would be hard pressed to supply an appropriate ending for the expression "meek as a ———."

The fact that we immediately associate meekness with mice—for "mouse," it goes without saying, is the proper conclusion of this simile—reveals something noteworthy about the culture in which we live. It implies that we put a low premium on the quality of meekness. In the grand scheme of things, a mouse is a skittish and weak creature. It frightens easily, retreats before aggressors, darts hither and yon in a seemingly never-ending strategy of evasion and escape. All it wishes is to be left alone to pursue its rather pedestrian interests. It has no greater ambition than safety.

In spite of (or perhaps because of) its timidity, some of us see mice as cute creatures. But when the same characteristics that endear a cuddly mouse to us are ascribed to a person, the transfer is never complimentary. To say that a person is "meek as a mouse" is to insinuate that he's morally, or at least psychologically, flawed. In the popular lexicon, someone who's mousy or meek is weak-willed and spiritless to the point of cowardice. He's a milquetoast who lets people walk all over him, a spineless wall-flower with neither the emotional nor physical moxie to cut it in the rough-and-tumble of life. We may pity a meek person, and occasionally even go out of our way to encourage a sense of pride or assertiveness in him, but our coaching is typically tinged with irritated contempt: *What does it take to get you to stand on your own two feet? Don't you realize how pathetic you are? Are you a man or a mouse?*

Now, none of this comes as any surprise. Our culture trains us to value go-getting, stalwart individuals who push and shove their way to the top. Meek people usually end up at the tail end of the societal food chain. What *is* surprising, however, is that many Christians share the cultural contempt for the quality of meekness. Of course, we all know that the New Testament places a high premium on meekness, and that Jesus—himself described as a meek man—explicitly praises it in the Sermon on the Mount.

But we Christians are no different from other humans in our talent for compartmentalizing dissonant attitudes in order to accommodate them. When we enter our "churchy" or "pious" compartments, we praise the blessedness of meekness. But when we leave the pew for our "real world" secular compartments, we despise the very quality we earlier lauded.

What this means is that many of us concur to one extent or another with Nietzsche's disdainful repudiation of the Christian virtue of meekness. We might not be consciously aware of our agreement; we may, in fact, never have read a word of Nietzsche. But for all that, we're in his camp. For Nietzsche's writings both articulate and feed the general cultural conviction that meek persons have the lowly status of mice.

The Mouse Who Couldn't Roar

Nietzsche's criticisms of the Christian way are widely scattered throughout his books. Some of them, although ultimately misguided, are brilliantly original and psychologically penetrating. Others, especially those written toward the end of his life, tend to be shrill one-liners. But one of the threads that binds them all together is the unshakable conviction that Christianity's espousal of spiritual meekness shows it up as a religion created *by* slaves *for* slaves.

The good news proclaimed by Christianity is that Christ came to free us from the bondage of our own waywardness. But so far as Nietzsche is concerned, this is "idle falsehood and deception," a "great unholy lie," the "most fatal[ly] seductive lie that has yet existed."[1] Far from bestowing liberation, the Christian message of meekness actually stymies our most basic and "healthy" instincts, binding us in shackles of pathological guilt, frustrated envy, and profound self-hatred that over the last two thousand years have proven well-nigh unbreakable. Nietzsche would reject as dead wrong Karl Rahner's claim that the purpose of Christianity is to encourage personhood. On the contrary, Christianity mutates us into subhuman creatures—into a bipedal species of mice, if you will.

Nietzsche's insistence that Christian meekness is a perverse form of slavery can be appreciated only when read against the backdrop of his notorious distinction between "master" and "slave" types. "Masters" are fully developed humans. "Slaves," on the other hand, are pathetically broken caricatures of what true humanness is all about.

A "master" is a man (I use the masculine pronoun deliberately, since Nietzsche's misogyny apparently precludes women from this rank) who has the indomitable "soul of a proud Viking," iron-muscled and iron-willed.[2] He recognizes and embraces a surging instinct deep within—what Nietzsche calls the "will to power"—to assert his individuality by taking charge of his existence and refusing to march to anyone's drum but his own. The master is a strong and unafraid "blond beast" who exultantly throws himself into life. His primary goal is to exist as passionately and intensely as he can, collecting experiences like a miser hoards coins.

In loosing the reins of his passions and allowing his deepest instinctual urges to surface, the master frequently scandalizes the conventional world. But what of it? The blond beast is self-sufficiently autonomous and contemptuously superior to the petty values endorsed by the common run of humans, the slaves whom Nietzsche also refers to as "herd-men." The master has no need of these slavish norms because he possesses the courage and resolve to create his own values. "The noble type of man experiences *itself* as determining values; it does not need approval; it judges 'what is harmful to me is harmful in itself';...It is value-creating."[3]

This self-bestowed moral autonomy gives the master a godlike freedom. He neither needs nor seeks outside approval for the unabashed indulgence of his passions. He dwells in an "exalted" state of "faith" in himself and "pride" in his courage, and therefore is "fundamentally hostile" to any creed or philosophy that tries to defend "selflessness." This spineless value he leaves to the "cowardly," "anxious," and "petty" herd-men, whose meekness he rightly "despises."[4] These annoying insects can buzz down their crooked path. He'll follow his own straight and narrow high road. But let the herd-men beware: The master will not allow them to interfere with the exercise of his will to power. If they leave him alone, he'll ignore them with the indifference of majestic superiority. But if they get in his way, he'll swat them without a trace of compunction.

So much for the master. What of the slave? He's a cringing, poltroonish mouse, utterly lacking the inner resources—the will to power—to transform himself into a master. Too weak and spiritless to stand on his own and carve out a destiny for himself, too "stupid" and "easy to deceive" to know what's in his best interests, he chooses instead to cling to the herd, anonymously burying himself in its safely conventional norms and values.[5] Thus a slave *deserves* to be a slave, because he's suited for nothing better than servitude. Freedom, in fact, is the last thing he really wants. Like all natural-born slaves, he peevishly resists self-determination and individuality. It's much more comfortable to be told what to think and do—to be, in short, manipulated.

If freedom is one of the slave's hobgoblins, intense feeling or passion is another. The blond beast's chest-thumping enthusiasm for raw life isn't for the likes of him. What the slave wants above all else is a staid, unruffled existence in which pleasures and pains are modulated to a nonthreatening level. Volcanic peaks of hot love or explosive hatred upset his bovine complacency, and the slightest hint of them sends him racing back to the flatlands of safely subdued feelings. Tepid love and sluggish resentment are more suited to his weak constitution. So the slave is as anemic in emotions as he is stupid in intellect and emasculated in will. At the end of the day, all he's really good for is meekly running with the herd.

Even so, the slave carries within him a hidden desire, one that so threatens his neurotic need for the safety of the herd that he buries it deeply in his psyche: he yearns to be a master. Every mouse secretly wants to roar like a lion; every milquetoast fantasizes about being a sand-kicking bully on the beach. How wonderful it would be just once to don the armor of a master and bestride the world, to thumb one's nose at the herd and strut one's independence!

This secret desire to be what he cannot creates an unbearable tension within the slave. By nature he's a cowardly, stupid drone who requires the regulated anonymity of the hive. Occasionally, however, he longs to break free of constraints and soar off on his own. But his impotence is so entrenched that these fantasies terrify as much as titillate. So he quickly retreats from them, and in that moment of flight, even he—poor self-deceived creature though he is—catches a glimpse of just how thoroughly despicable he is. The awareness of his pathetic nature cannot but afflict him with an occasional stab of frustration and self-loathing. Then he truly feels the fetters biting into his wrists and knows himself too weakly indecisive to strike them off.

What recourse does he have? Nietzsche gives us a clue by posing a question: "Suppose the violated, oppressed, suffering, unfree, who are uncertain of themselves and weary, moralize: what will their moral valuations have in common?"[6] Nietzsche thinks the obvious answer is that the values such slaves would latch onto, as the core of their moral and religious beliefs, inevitably would reflect the only qualities they're capable of: cowardice, subservience, submission—in a word, *meekness*. A human can't long endure self-loathing. If he doesn't discover a way out, he explodes. The slave finds his outlet by elevating unhappy necessity to the status of virtue. Since he can never attain what he secretly aspires to, he fools himself into thinking that what he has is eminently desirable. He condemns the proud self-sufficiency and passionate exuberance of the master as moral and spiritual failings—as "sins"—and contrasts them with the good or holy "virtues" of self-denial and instinct-repression. This allows the slave to interpret his meekness as spiritually superior to the master's strength. Such a perverse "transvaluation" of meekness from contemptible flaw to praiseworthy virtue, which Nietzsche sees as the slave's last-ditch defense against self-hatred and impotent envy, is Christianity's spiritual center of gravity. The mouse who can't roar makes a religion out of squeaking.

For Nietzsche, then, the Christian valuation of meekness is the direct consequence of a "popular uprising, the revolt of [an] underprivileged" class whose inherent weakness forces it to resort to chicanery and self-deception.[7] The mere possibility that a slavish quality such as meekness could be "blessed" fills him with amazement. It's a "mode of thought," he says, "typical of a suffering and feeble species of man," a species comfortable only with a "religion for sufferers" that praises weakness as a virtue and condemns strength as a vice.[8] But the "moral castration" preached by such a religion is as ludicrous as it is unnatural:

> To demand of strength that it should *not* express itself as strength, that it should *not* be a desire to overcome, a desire to throw down, a desire to become master, a thirst for enemies and resistances and triumphs, is just as absurd as to demand of weakness that it should express itself as strength.[9]

Absurd and unnatural as it is, however, meekness has become so thoroughly transvalued by "lying little abortions of bigots"— that is, Christians—that they shamelessly flaunt their impotence by taking for themselves a god who epitomizes weakness. Not for them the majestically heroic gods of Valhalla. Instead, they scurry to a suffering servant, a god despised and rejected, a mouse-god who, like themselves, meekly repudiates masculine strength and instinctual passion by turning the other cheek. The *castrati* worship a *castrato*, a deity made in their own miserable likeness. Little wonder, says Nietzsche, that the central image of this religion of slaves is the cross, a degrading symbol of defeat that "takes the side of idiots...², utters a curse on the spirit, [and urges] rancor against the gifted, learned, [and] spiritually independent"!¹⁰

We get the gods we deserve, and the slave deserves no better deity than a slavish one.

"If the Shoe Fits..."

The furious intensity of Nietzsche's assault against Christian meekness leaves one breathless, doesn't it? It's tempting to shield one's head and shoulders from his relentless pounding by crying out that he's an obvious madman who's gotten everything backwards. But I would suggest that only part of our discomfort arises from the sheer brutality of his attack. Some of it also comes from the sad fact that a few of Nietzsche's shots hit distressingly close to home. If we hope to grow in our appreciation of *genuine* Christian meekness, we must be honest enough to admit two possibilities: First, that many of us are more sympathetic to Nietzsche's contemptuous repudiation of meekness than we consciously acknowledge; second, that many of us who believe we value Christian meekness may only do so, as Nietzsche suggests, out of a defensive need to justify personal cowardice or resentment. These *are* harsh words. But if the shoe fits in even the slightest way, we must face up to it before we can move on.

We've already seen one way in which Nietzsche's words strike home: the tendency many of us have to praise meekness in one context but despise it in others. It's perfectly okay for children to hear about Jesus-meek-and-mild in church school—maybe it'll even improve their behavior at home—or for their parents to sit through the occasional sermon on turning the other cheek. But the unhappy fact that many of us draw a clear line between tolerating pious (and no-risk) chatter about meekness on Sundays, and actually valuing (or even exercising) meekness in the practical world during the rest of the week, suggests that we, like Nietzsche, find something "absurd" and "unnatural" about it.

Who among us can honestly say that we want our kids to carry the Sunday School lesson of meekness with them onto the playground, much less into the eat-or-be-eaten workplace that awaits them when they grow into adults? Who among us isn't irritably impatient with the talented relative who simply won't take advantage of his or her gifts to "make something of herself"? Who among us doesn't suspect, at least sometimes, that meekness is an unnatural repression of passionate instinct? And what do we really want from our political leaders? Do we want them to emulate Jesus-meek-and-mild, or do we want them to go for the throat when it comes to looking out for our interests?

I'm not saying that genuine Christian meekness obliges our children to allow themselves to be terrorized by school bullies, or that it excuses talented relatives and national leaders from making good use of their gifts or showing firmness when firmness is appropriate. Rather, my point is that we too frequently assume, as Nietzsche did, that meekness in the real world is a frightened, mouse-like timidity that inhibits us from being all we can be. If we have such a negative opinion of "practical" meekness, how wide of the mark is it to conclude that we don't really value "spiritual" meekness all that much either? We've been socialized by our religious upbringing to pay lip service to it, but the real test of our convictions is whether we try to live what we say. And sad experience suggests that many of us fail that test miserably. Deep down, far beneath all our pious platitudes, we find meekness absurd and unnatural.

Given that our disdain of "practical" meekness necessarily says something about our opinion of "spiritual" meekness as well, it's likely that the "churchy" compartment we try to keep separate from the real-world compartment is also tainted by our Nietzschean distrust of meekness, although in subtle, scarcely noticeable ways. True, we piously praise spiritual meekness when nothing much is at stake. But when it comes to "important" issues within the church, we sing a different tune.

Many of us, for example, don't really want a parish priest who exemplifies Christian meekness (or at least what we understand Christian meekness to be) in his attitudes and counsel. We want a go-getter, a CEO-padre who has the smarts and assertiveness— a sort of "sanctified" will to power—to grow the congregation and the budget, and whose spiritual direction isn't going to be larded with tiresome lectures on self-denial and humility. Leave that stuff to cloistered monks and nuns. We live in the real world, and we need a priest who appreciates old-fashioned common sense!

If we're not especially careful, we can even fall into the bog that traps many evangelical Protestants. We can convince ourselves that what's really needed in this "fallen" day and age is a zealous, two-fisted, in-your-face Christianity that noisily punches its way to center stage in order to "redeem" the world. Even thoughtful contemporary Christians such as C.S. Lewis have defended this sort of belligerently no-nonsense approach. (Fortunately, Lewis quickly grew out of it.)

I don't wish to claim that only impractical bumblers or dour ascetics make good priests, or that Christians ought not to share the good news with the world. My suggestion instead is that our underlying distrust of meekness as an absurd and unnatural enslavement can mutate even our most intentional efforts to be good Christians into an unseemly militancy (as if there isn't something immediately suspect about the expression "militant Christianity"). Once more, this isn't really surprising. We may try to segregate our lives into airtight secular and churchy compartments, but we can never really succeed. Deep-seated fidelity to the will to power inevitably expresses itself in all arenas of existence.

Painful as it may be, then, honest self-examination suggests that many of us, sometimes and in some ways, silently agree with the Nietzschean claim that meekness is an unnatural and harmful repression of healthily energetic instinct, and that it betokens a hamstrung ineffectiveness in the world. This bombshell, at least, has our name on it. But there's still another way in which Nietzsche's criticisms hit closer to home than we might expect or wish to admit. It has to do with his insistence that Christian meekness is a ruse for coping with frustrated and resentful impotence.

We humans are astoundingly versatile creatures, able to adapt ourselves to any number of unfriendly environments. Such adaptability is a necessary condition for our survival both as individuals and as a species. When it comes to the *external* environment, we survive by accurately appraising the situation, determining what we need to do in order to get by, and adjusting accordingly. But we dwell in another environment as well, the *internal* one of moods, emotions, ideas, and temperament, and this environment can sometimes be more harshly inhospitable than anything the outside world throws at us. Ideally, the survival strategies we practice in this inner place parallel the ones we use in the outside world: an objectively honest assessment of the situation, and consequent readjustment. This, after all, is the method of psychotherapy. We confront the neuroses that threaten our internal equilibrium, admit temperamental weaknesses or trauma-induced flaws, and try to work around them.

But sometimes the neuroses that determine the contours of our inner landscape are simply too threatening to face forthrightly. So we fall into a psychological survival strategy that's less than ideal, but nonetheless allows us to cope: the self-deception of rationalization. We relabel and redefine our own failings in order to make them less of a burden to our conscience. For example, we excuse self-absorbed and vaunting ambition by convincing ourselves that it's really conscientious dedication to our work; defend the busybody habit of interfering in the lives of others by calling it benevolent concern; or justify our inability to cultivate responsible relationships by persuading ourselves that we're "free spirits" who need room to soar. Psychological rationalization, then, is very much like what Nietzsche called the "transvaluation." When we adapt to unpleasant internal environments by rationalizing, we cope with our inner demons by bestowing on them the status of virtues.

One of the most effective ways of coping with flaws in the internal environment, as Nietzsche correctly discerned, is stamping them with a religious *nihil obstat*. When we do this, we convince ourselves that those motives and character traits we uneasily sense as dubious in fact are holy and pleasing to God. Intolerance becomes zeal in the service of the Church, harsh judgmentalism rolls over into righteousness, pharisaic nit-picking masquerades as fidelity to the law. All sorts of selfish acts and unsavory motives are justified—and done so with unabashed "sincerity"—in the name of religion.

Seen in this light, Nietzsche's claim that Christian meekness is a rationalization for slavish timidity should give us pause for serious thought. One needn't buy his uncompromising condemnation of meekness to acknowledge the possibility that what claims to be a virtuous turning-of-the-cheek is sometimes really a disguise for run-of-the-mill timidity. Surely there's a palpable distinction between the meekness Jesus preached in the Sermon on the Mount and the "meekness" of a moral or physical coward. The first is cultivated out of an earnest desire to please God, whatever the cost. The second, although it masquerades as service to God, is actually a selfish strategy for saving one's own skin or, less dramatically, avoiding hassles that upset one's comfort level.

As Nietzsche saw, this kind of posing may provide some immediate insulation, but ultimately leads to frustration and resentment. The reason is obvious: Because the meekness is only a self-protective facade, there's no real congruity between the outer mask of meekness and the inner insecurity it desperately tries to conceal. The upshot is a spiritual and psychic splintering that breeds a chronic sense of angry grievance. Thomas Merton captures this unhappy state of affairs in a poignant entry from one of his private diaries. "I am humble [or meek] after a fashion," he confesses, "but when people cross me up, although I give in, I am interiorly too sardonic and tough about it, and I resist, and try to get even by being secretly contemptuous."[11] Those of us who practice the false meekness of rationalization are prone to the same irresolution as Merton. What separates him from many of us is his painfully honest appraisal of his condition.

That the practice of Christian meekness can be tainted to one degree or another in this way, even by those who sincerely believe they practice it, is both a frightening and real possibility.

When coupled with the fact that many of us harbor a Nietzschean suspicion about the absurdity and unnaturalness of meekness, the need to face our own ambivalence and to become clear about our motives is even more striking. Nietzsche's condemnation of meekness is, I believe, incorrect. But his challenge demands to be taken seriously because it articulates many of our own confusions and misconceptions about Christian meekness. Now that we can confess the plank in our own eyes, we're ready to examine with clear vision and open hearts what scripture and tradition have to tell us about genuine meekness.

Clearing the Ground

First we need to defuse the bombs Nietzsche lobbed at Christian meekness. This isn't as difficult as it may seem (although I don't mean by this to trivialize either the strength or relevance of his challenge), because scripture makes it clear that authentic meekness is anything but the contemptible mousiness he and so many of us take it to be. Let's begin with the claim that meekness is an absurd and unnatural suffocation of "healthy" instinctual drives.

"Blessed are the meek," says Jesus (Matt 5:5). This is the third of the nine Beatitudes with which he began the Sermon on the Mount. Taken together, the Beatitudes are the core of Jesus' spiritual teaching. Everything else in the Sermon, and indeed all of Jesus' other instructions recorded in the Gospels, are glosses on them.

Everyone recognizes that the Beatitudes are a prescription for a godly life. But what's frequently overlooked is that they're also autobiographical. In giving them to the disciples, Jesus describes, point by point, who and what he is. His implicit message is: "Be like me, as I am like the Father. I'm blessed with poverty of spirit, sorrow, meekness, hunger for righteousness (and so on), and these qualities express my at-one-ment with God. If you imitate me, you too can grow in Godlikeness." It's significant that the word we translate as *blessed* is *makarios,* a Greek term suggesting a state of completion or fulfillment enjoyed by the gods. The more we cultivate openness to the beatific virtues, the closer we approximate the fullness of God expressed in his Son. The teaching Jesus gives us in the Sermon on the Mount, in other words, is *himself.* This is only as it should be, since Jesus is the Word incarnate, a flesh-and-blood Teaching.

This immediately clues us in to a crucial fact about meekness: it is holy, a way of being that originates from and reflects the nature of God himself. That's why scripture refers to it as a gift of the Spirit (Gal 5:23), of election (Col 3:12), and of calling (Eph 4:2). Consequently, there's no question of it being either "absurd" or "unnatural." On the contrary, expressing as it does the holiness of God, meekness is preeminently meaningful (because it leads to *makarios*) as well as totally natural for beings created in God's likeness, even if it appears quite otherwise to the eyes of the world.

A careful reading of scripture discloses yet another characteristic of genuine meekness that puts the lie to our Nietzschean perceptions of it. We've already seen that Jesus' implication in the third Beatitude is that he exemplifies meekness; elsewhere (Matt 11:29), he claims meekness for himself in more direct terms. The only other biblical character to whom meekness is explicitly attributed is Moses: "Now the man Moses was very meek, more than all men that were on the face of the earth" (Num 12:3).

The fact that scripture singles out Jesus and Moses as persons of meekness is illuminating. Both of them were charismatic leaders with clearly defined missions; both were astonishingly effective in accomplishing what they set out to achieve; and their success strongly suggests that both possessed remarkable self-knowledge: they knew their strengths and weaknesses, and consequently were free both of the self-deception of rationalization and the lack of resoluteness that bedeviled Thomas Merton—and still bedevils us. They knew who they were and what they were about.

What this tells us is that genuine meekness is neither the timidly mousy ineffectiveness for which so many of us feel silent contempt, nor a psychological strategy for hiding from our own cowardice or listlessness. Instead, meekness is a spiritual strength that bestows clarity on who we really are, harmonizes inner intention and outward comportment, and empowers us to undertake heroic deeds in the world. The strength bestowed by meekness certainly isn't the kind of self-generated chutzpah that Nietzsche admires in his "master" race, or that we praise in will-to-powered individuals who fight their way to the top of the pecking order. Instead, as we'll see shortly, it's a strength that comes from a relinquishment of the will to power's incessant drive to dominate.

Scripture reveals something else about genuine meekness, one that's particularly startling for those of us who have bought to one degree or another Nietzsche's claim that the meek person is a slave. We've already seen that the quality of meekness liberates us from both psychological self-deceptions about our inner states as well as from our oppressive powerlessness to harmonize intent and act. But two scriptural texts additionally assure us that meekness brings external as well as internal freedom. One comes from the psalmist (37:11): "...the meek shall possess the land, and delight themselves in abundant prosperity." The other is from the third Beatitude itself, where Jesus promises that the meek "shall inherit the earth." The Hebrew and Greek words that we render in English as "prosperity," "land," and "earth" carry no hint of otherworldly riches and domains. There's no suggestion in them of heavenly "pie in the sky"; instead, their unmistakable intent is that the reward of meekness is tangibly here-and-now, in this life, on this planet.

This is hardly the plight of a slave dispossessed of everything that makes life worth living and abjectly dependent on the whims of a master. Rather, the words of both Jesus and the psalmist suggest an existence in which the truly good things of life are plentifully available. The meek person is not enslaved by wants, either external or internal ones, for the simple reason, which we'll explore more fully later, that his meekness has brought him a poverty replete with riches unimagined by Nietzschean masters or power-hungry go-getters.

These preliminary remarks reveal that those of us inclined to accept a Nietzschean repudiation of meekness do so, as did he, because we fundamentally misunderstand what the scriptures mean by it. Nietzsche and his followers are correct up to a certain point, but no further. It's true that the world dismisses meekness as an absurd and unnatural repression of instinct, but it's false to assume that authentic meekness is either absurd or unnatural. While it's equally true that we can deceive ourselves into believing that our own timid ineffectiveness and spiritlessness is genuine meekness, the real thing—the meekness practiced by Jesus and Moses—brings self-clarity, resoluteness, and strength. Finally, even though slavish temperaments can display a mousy servility that convention identifies with meekness, the genuinely meek person is not enslaved because the riches bestowed by meekness liberate him from unfulfilled wants. As I said earlier, we do well to take Nietzsche's challenge seriously, but only to safeguard ourselves from falling into the same misconceptions about meekness that confused him.

The Beast Within

We've seen what Christian meekness is *not*, and along the way we've caught a few glimpses of what it is. Now we're ready to explore these hints more fully, and we can begin by taking a look at the meaning of the Greek word commonly translated as *meek*.

In the third Beatitude, Jesus says that meek persons, or *praeis*, are blessed, or *makarios*. *Praeis* is linked to the adjective *praus*, "meek," which in turn comes from the noun *praotes*, "meekness." Although the word *praus* is rich in connotation, it typically was used in the Greek world to describe the condition of a domesticated animal. A feral creature is dangerously unpredictable because it's beyond the bounds of any constraint. But when habituated to discipline—when its untamed will is subjugated by the will of another—it acquires *praotes*. A wild mustang becomes *praus* once it submits to bit and bridle.

Frightening as wild animals can be, none of them match the ferocity of the human beast. Few animals maim or kill for the sheer pleasure of it. The human creature, as both shameful personal experience and the sorry history of the race suggest, seems possessed by an almost uncontrollable lust to dominate and destroy others. The Greeks were as aware of this unhappy tendency as we today are, and it was only a short step for them to see that *praotes* in humans was even more desirable than *praotes* in animals. So what began as a descriptive term in husbandry eventually took on the status of a prescriptive term in ethics. *Praotes* became a virtue of the individual who has disciplined his wild and unruly urges. Thus a "meek" person is one who tames the savage beast within.

But what is this beast that the virtuous person seeks to tame? It's nothing less than what Nietzsche admires as will to power: unbridled self-assertion, the utterly egoistic drive to run roughshod over anyone perceived as a threat to personal gratification and aggrandizement. In this regard, the beast is very much like what Freud in the twentieth century called the *id*: that narcissistic part of the human psyche that incessantly craves to satisfy its hunger by taking *what* it wants *when* it wants. The id brooks no opposition to its desires, accepts no constraints on its urges. Its only reference point is itself, and if it senses the slightest opposition, it lashes out savagely to protect its interests. Seizure, control, satiation: these are the imperatives of the "blond beast" of self-will.[12]

It follows that the trademark of an untamed or unmeek person is a ferocious rapacity that values the untrammeled acquisition of power, incendiary passion, and instant gratification above all else. When the full flow of these "healthy" instincts is hindered in any way, the predictable outburst is either violently retaliatory anger or peevishly burning resentment.

The authors of the New Testament were well aware of the violence bred by unchecked self-will, and generally referred to it either as *phumos* or *orge*. *Phumos* (whence we derive expressions like "to fume with anger") is a spontaneous explosion of the thwarted will to power, the seething rage that boils up when the beast within thinks its sovereignty has been crossed in one way or another. Luke, for example, uses the word to describe the blind anger that overwhelmed worshippers in Nazareth's synagogue when Jesus declared himself the Messiah foretold by the prophet Isaiah (4:28). Luke again uses *phumos* to characterize the whirlwind of fury Paul's denunciation of idolatry churned up in the Ephesians (Acts 19:28).

Orge, on the other hand, carries a connotation of deliberately chosen peevishness and resentment. In *phumos*, rage is a sort of impulsive madness that comes upon a person. But in *orge*, rage seems to be a somewhat more self-aware act, one that's intentionally directed toward the object of wrath for the conscious purpose of defeat and destruction. The apostle James uses *orge* when he advises his brethren to be "slow to anger" (James 1:19), the implication being that the wrath he refers to is at least to some extent calculative and hence within an individual's control.

When non-Christian Greek philosophers thought of the unmeek wrath bred by overreaching self-will, what they typically had in mind was something like James's *orge*. It naturally followed that they believed the raging beast could be tamed by an internal effort on the part of the angry person. Aristotle, for example, taught that the way to control anger was to exercise rational moderation in one's desire for self-advancement. A prudent assessment of one's own strengths and weaknesses, coupled with an objective appreciation of the distinction between foolish and legitimate desires, would eventually result in a psychic equilibrium between excessive anger and excessive angerlessness. Thus the beast within could be tamed by a regimen of rational self-control.[13]

But from a Christian perspective, things aren't quite this simple. In the first place, calling on the will to control the will is a bit like trying to quench a flame by flinging oil on it. Anger, even the deliberative kind suggested by *orge*, flares up precisely because the self has taken its own will as sovereign and bitterly resents anything it senses to be a contravention of its prerogatives. Attempts to rein in the will through an effort of will only strengthen its overblown presumption of ultimate authority. If unmeekness is ultimately traceable to an already hyperactive will, it doesn't seem likely that meekness can be attained by yet another strenuous act of the will. How can a wild beast tame its own nature by exercising and hence toning up the very muscles that make it wild?

The second reason to be dubious about the self's ability to police its imperious will and thus curb its tendency to thwarted rage is that the anger it experiences is spontaneous *phumos* just as frequently as splenetic *orge*. But *phumos* is by definition an uncontrollable explosion that tidal-waves over an individual. It's neither planned nor self-aware; it takes a person by surprise and carries him or her off in blind fury. Even were it possible to wean oneself from calculated acts of *orge* through a sheer act of the will, it's difficult to see how such *bootstrapping* could also handle outbursts of *phumos*.

Such is certainly Paul's position in his epistle to the Romans, a document which, like the Sermon on the Mount, is as much autobiographical as theological. Paul spent a good portion of his life trying to tame the beast by laborious efforts at self-control. In his case, the regimen he practiced was a scrupulous fidelity to Torah, the Law. With steely determination, he willed himself to conform to the Commandments. His hard work brought in one or two paltry dividends. He was reckoned a virtuous man by his fellow Jews, and there's little doubt that his taxing efforts at self-discipline probably curbed his more ferocious tendencies toward *orge*.

But in spite of all this, Paul remained a passionately angry man—witness his savage persecution of the early followers of Jesus—windswept by irrational outbursts of *phumos*-fury that left nothing but wreckage in their wake. He sensed the beast within and struggled valiantly to tame it. Yet his best efforts fell short of the mark. Years later, recalling those early days, he described the terrible effects of his will to power in heartrending terms:

> So I find it to be a law that when I want to do right, evil lies close at hand. For I delight in the law of God, in my inmost self, but I see in my members another law at war with the law of my spirit and making me captive to the law of sin which dwells in my members. Wretched man that I am! Who will deliver me from this body of death? (Rom 7:21–24)

Paul's confession is significant because it pushes beyond the story of his own struggles toward two truths applicable to the spiritual life in general. The first is that the feral will to power enslaves, pushing and pulling us in directions *it* wants to go, stirring up a raging civil war that uses the soul as a battleground. The unmeek person, in other words, is a conscript, wretchedly pressed into the service of a megalomaniac general whose uncontrolled lust for conquest erupts in devastating fits of *phumos*.

The second spiritual truth Paul's words convey is what I've suggested already: the beast of self-will can't be tamed by will. Its impulses are too strong, its frenzy to dominate too intense. All efforts to take the beast in hand through sheer will-power only tighten its muscles and increase its appetite. When Paul desperately cries out for deliverance, he admits he can't save himself. Unmeekness can't be grafted onto meekness. The slave has neither the strength nor authority to strike off his chains. The situation seems hopeless.

And yet, it can't be. Jesus' Sermon on the Mount prescribes meekness as one of the chief spiritual virtues, and scripture promises (1 Cor 10:13) that God doesn't require more of us than we're able to deliver. The letter to Titus likewise insists that all Christians should be *praus* (3:2), and Paul—the same Paul who in Romans voiced such plaintive despair over his bondage—claims in another letter (2 Cor 10:1) to have finally broken through to *praotes*. So hopeless as the situation appears, there must be a way of taming the beast.

Blessed Poverty

Some wild beasts have such an indomitable will that a head-on confrontation with them is foolhardy. Just when we think we've got them cornered, they call up hidden reserves of strength and counterattack with a ferocity that leaves us dazed. Exhausted defeat—ours, not theirs—is the inevitable outcome.

But for all that, such beasts can be tamed. The trick is not to go after them in a frontal assault, but simply to walk away. Leave them in stunned perplexity and frustrated bloodlust. They'll roar and howl for a time, challenging us to sally forth and resume battle. But after a while, deprived of fresh kills, they languish from starvation. So it is with that most ferocious of all predators, self-will.

Walking away from a fight isn't something that comes easily to most of us. We've been conditioned from early childhood to stand up to bullies, demand our rights, refuse to throw in the towel when faced with adversity. Anything less, we're taught, is cowardice—"meekness."

But fighting only makes practical sense (whether it makes *moral* sense is another question altogether) if there's a reasonable chance of victory, and when it comes to subduing the will to power through an act of will, the deck is stacked against us. Even if we manage to curb the worst of our *orge*, *phumos* will inevitably defy our feeble stabs at self-discipline. No, the only sane course of action here is to acknowledge powerlessness and simply give up the struggle. This isn't cowardice, but rather a clear-headed and honest confession of our own limitations. It's the humility that comes from a recognition of our own impoverishment. And this impoverishment, if we but knew it, is a great blessing, because it's poverty that tames the beast.

Jesus tells us as much in the Sermon on the Mount when he designates "poverty of spirit" as the first Beatitude. Spiritual poverty is the blessing that grounds all other blessings, the gift that prepares us for all other gifts. In its absence, nothing is possible; with it, everything—including meekness—is.

The word that English translations of the first Beatitude render as "poor" is *ptoches*. *Ptoches* is a frightening term, derived from the verb *ptossein*, "to cower or crouch." In Greek, there are two words that can be rendered "poor." One, obviously, is *ptoches*; the other is *penes*. *Penes* refers to the condition of a person who barely has enough to get by, who lives precariously from hand to mouth. It's the situation of an unskilled day-laborer whose work brings him bread at the end of the day, but nothing more. *Ptoches*, on the other hand, refers to a state of utter destitution. A person who finds himself in this kind of poverty has absolutely no resources upon which to draw and no possibility of bootstrapping out of his situation. He lacks the skills and talents necessary to support himself, and the environment in which he dwells is relentlessly harsh. All he can do is crouch or cower in abject helplessness. This is the condition, for example, of a homeless street person or an abandoned child.

Ptoches typically refers to a state of physical or material destitution. But Jesus put a startlingly new spin on the word by using it to describe inner destitution—*ptochoi to pneumati*, "poor in spirit." Unspeakable as material destitution is, inner destitution is a hundredfold worse. The homeless person can always hope against hope that one day he'll find a way to turn the corner and come upon a less-harsh neighborhood. But the spiritually impoverished person carries his destitute environment within him. Whatever street he stumbles down leads to the same dead-end of squalor and misery. How does he escape from himself? Whichever way he turns, the same grimy alley of desolation stretches before him. He can race desperately pell-mell struggling to find a way out until he collapses in exhausted stupor. But he'll never run his way out of the alley.

The horror of spiritual destitution is precisely the condition Paul describes in his letter to the Romans: hopeless entrapment in the labyrinth of the beast. Paul tried to fight his way out by wielding Torah as a weapon, by trying to rout the beast of self-will and break through the maze with the battering ram of rigid conformity to the Law. But he discovered to his dismay that the more strenuously he fought the beast, the stronger it grew. Doubtlessly his struggles escalated as his sense of impotent despair grew: the final paroxysms of a drowning man. But eventually even Paul, doughty warrior though he was, had to acknowledge the helplessness of his situation and confess his own *ptoches*. And at that moment his anguished scream echoed throughout the labyrinth: *Wretched man that I am! Who will deliver me?* This inner destitution doesn't seem like much of a blessing, does it? But Jesus promises us otherwise, and a bit of reflection discloses his reasoning. A person suffering from material destitution eventually reaches the point where he or she knows she can do nothing to save herself. His or her best efforts have spiraled in one dismal failure after another until her will is so broken that she simply lacks either the energy or resolve to continue. She cowers in the alley, covers her head, and from the depths of her despair cries out for succor.

We who have exhausted ourselves fighting the beast reach a similar point. When spiritual exhaustion brings us to our knees and forces us to admit that we can't tame the creature through our own efforts; when we know ourselves to be without the vast reserves of stamina and endurance we once foolishly claimed as Nietzschean "masters"; when we realize that our conceit of self-control is not only false but destructive, engendering as it does an inner wasteland hostile to us but conducive to the beast's flourishing; when we're so sapped of energy that we're capable of neither *orge* nor *phumos*; when, in short, the last vestiges of our arrogant will to power are stripped from us: only then are we brought so low that we cry out with Paul for a deliverer and open ourselves to aid from the outside. We destitutely huddle in the labyrinth of our souls and wait.

The street person can never be confident that his or her wretched plea for help will be heard. Relying upon the kindness of strangers is a chancy business. The world, alas, is more populated with indifferent passers-by than Good Samaritans. But Jesus says in the Sermon on the Mount that the person of spiritual *ptoches* who cries for aid will be blessed. Desperate pleas for bread will not be mocked with stones. God will respond to a broken and contrite heart, just as God responded to Paul by restoring his sight, sanity, and soul during the black days and nights that followed his collapse on the road to Damascus.

Mind you, it's not that our destitution brings an absentee God scurrying back home to pull our chestnuts out of the fire. God has always been present to us. Paul sensed this even in the depths of his destitution. He dimly discerned God's whisper in his "inmost self," he tells us, but the loud and incessant clamor of his arrogant self-will by and large deafened him to it. To hear God's still, small voice, we must listen for it. But listening is only possible when we become quiet—when our will ceases its noisy and self-important maneuvering, when we finally acknowledge defeat and lay down our arms. "To listen to God," says Merton, "means, first of all, to recognize our helplessness, our stupidity, our blindness and ignorance."[14] Only then, when we fall abjectly quiet and await in silence, are we receptive to the ever-present God. "Only the one," as André Louf writes, "who touches rock-bottom, the ground of his being and of his deepest feelings, can be spontaneously and deeply, truly humble."[15] This deep receptivity isn't something we can cultivate through an act of will; trying to do so only feeds the beast. It comes to us in but one way: as a gift born of *ptoches*. The thirteenth-century Beguine nun Mechthild of Magdeburg expresses this insight beautifully when she imagines God speaking these words to a soul in destitute despair:

Wherever I bestowed special favors,
I always sought out the lowest, most insignificant, and
    most unknown place for them.
The highest mountains on earth cannot receive the reve-
    lations of my favors
Because the course of my Holy Spirit flows by nature
    downhill.[16]

Blessed indeed are the poor in spirit, for only they are broken
enough to cease doing battle with the beast; only they are empty
enough to receive the waters of salvation.

Accepting the Gift

Ptoches isn't meekness, but it *is* a necessary condition for it. For
ptoches is a process of stripping down that eventually tames the
beast of angry self-will by starving it to the point of submission.
Only after the beast has been subdued in this way are we liberated from its dominion over us. Paul refers to this relinquishment
of self-control on our part as a participation in the horror of the
crucifixion. But after the ordeal on the cross comes rebirth.

We know that our old self was crucified with [Jesus] so
that the sinful body [self-will] might be destroyed, and
we might no longer be enslaved to sin. But if we have
died with Christ, we believe that we shall also live with
him....So you must consider yourselves dead to sin and
alive to God in Christ Jesus. (Rom 6:6–8, 11)

What does it mean to "live in Christ"? Simply this: when we
quit struggling with the beast long enough to recognize the utter
poverty of our own will, we're released to focus on the indescrib-
able richness of God's. We no longer struggle to take control of

our lives, but acknowledge that those lives are exactly where they've always been: in God's hands. With this awareness comes the realization that this is the best place for them to be. The newly found receptivity to the divine presence in our "inmost self" awakens us to the fact that loss of our self-image as a "master" brings genuine clarity about our true identity, that dependence on God constitutes real freedom, that the weakness of a broken will is our strength, and that the impoverishment of spirit floods us with riches. Self-knowledge, liberty, strength, wealth: each of these, as we saw a few pages back, is a gift of the spirit that blesses the person of true meekness. Let's examine them in turn.

We achieve clarity about our true identity when we live in Christ because we recognize that our old way of seeing ourselves was false. We fancied ourselves radically self-sufficient conquistadors, Nietzschean masters able to bulldoze our way through the world and even scale the heavens on sheer will power. Conquest, acquisition, gratification—in a word, *power*: these were the values through which the old self established its identity. But as Henri Nouwen once wisely observed, "to reach that inner sanctum where God's voice can be heard and obeyed is not easy if you are always called outward."[17] When poverty breaks the restless self-will that we so arrogantly worshipped in ourselves, we recognize the truth behind Nouwen's words: that our true identity is founded not on our incessantly outward-moving will, but on the will of the inmost-dwelling Spirit. We discover, as Paul did, that our true identity is not the master-self, but the Christ-self (Gal 2:20).

The freedom of living in Christ follows from the self-clarity it brings. The old self's foolishly proud confidence that it was in charge of the beast enslaved us in an escalating chaos of destructive will. No person at the beck and call of self-will is truly free, because self-will inevitably feeds the very passions that assail us. But when self-will exhausts itself and drops its conceit of autonomy, the tranquil peace of God takes its place, and this peace is *genuine* freedom: freedom from self-important ambition, freedom from the egoistic demand to dominate events and persons, freedom from the "healthy" instincts that control our every waking moment. "What liberty there would be in desiring nothing for myself!" writes Merton. "Once everything is God's, life becomes easy and simple....As soon as you cease to worry about your spurious importance and remember that God is all-important, life becomes a joy."[18]

This joyful freedom only comes when we acknowledge our dependence on God, and we only do that when we confess ourselves too weak-willed to make it on our own. Paul discovered that God's power is made perfect in weakness. The loss of arrogance that frees us from bondage is the source of true strength, because it opens us up to and grounds us in the majestic unassailability of the Divine. In surrendering our will to God's, we become the agents through which God's liberating power is released on earth. "For when I am weak, then I am strong" (2 Cor 12:10). When we live in Christ, we participate, as did he, in a strength that enables us to accept hardship, mockery, persecution, and even death with good grace and hope born of the conviction that we're invulnerable. We may suffer, and we will die. But we cannot perish.

Finally, as Jesus promised in both the first and third Beatitudes, the absolute poverty that allows us to live in Christ in fact makes us inexhaustibly wealthy. A person is "poor" only when he's unable to attain or hold onto those things necessary for his survival and well-being. Seen in this light, it's clear that the truly "poor" person is the Nietzschean master who scurries around in a ceaseless and futile race to carve out a secure niche for himself in the world. He can never attain all that he craves, and there's always the possibility that a stronger master will come along one day to rob him. But the person who lives in Christ possesses once and for all everything he could desire, even if his material state is one of penury. Living water and the bread of life is his, now and for all time. He truly has been given the gift of the Kingdom and, once his, it is his forever. As Paul came to realize, "neither death, nor life, nor angels, nor principalities, nor things present, nor things to come, nor powers, nor height, nor depth, nor anything else in all creation," can steal away the pearl of great price (Rom 8:38–39). So what more could such a person possibly want? And in wanting nothing but what he has, he is immeasurably rich.

When our own arrogant foolishness knocks us to our knees in the alley of spiritual destitution, we cease our futile battle with the beast, acknowledge our helplessness, and wait in the silence of utter exhaustion. Then the God who is always present in our inmost self can begin the work of restoration. When we feel his Spirit moving on the black waters of our despair, we—like our father Paul—are overawed with a gratitude and humility that forever more colors both our inner resolutions and our outer comportment. For we know with dreadful certainty that the clarity, freedom, strength, and wealth given us by God are utterly gratuitous, that we've neither done nor could ever do anything to deserve them. We accept the gift in fear and trembling, not understanding why it's been given, but knowing full well that without it we're lost. And we pledge ourselves—not in an act of self-assertion, but of trusting submission—to be worthy of the gift.

This is Christian meekness.

Living the Gift

Meekness is a gift from God that enables us to consciously and intentionally accept the Word engrafted forever in our hearts (Jas 1:21), and to live our calling to be branches of the sacred Vine. As we saw earlier, the nine Beatitudes function on one level as Jesus' self-description. His invitation to us in the Sermon on the Mount, then, is really to imitate his life and person. This is as it should be, for the heart and soul of Christian spirituality is precisely *imitatio Christi*: a steady growth in the engrafted Word that advances us toward that state of *makarios* wherein our wills unify with the Christ-will.

Living the gift of meekness, as St. Bernard reminds us in the epigraph to this chapter, means sinking more and more deeply into the gentle humbleness of Christ, in whom God mysteriously self-emptied, until that humbleness becomes second nature; humbly refusing to put ourselves before others, not out of false modesty, but from genuine gratitude for our essential poverty; turning the other cheek, not out of timidity, but from the knowledge that God's power and freedom is expressed in our patient forbearance; and owning up to our own helplessness, before both God and others, in the trust that our helplessness extends the divine invitation to *makarios* to a world that "waits with eager longing for the revealing of the sons [and daughters] of God" (Rom 8:19). Living the gift of meekness means a radical surrender of ourselves in all walks of life, not merely the ones in which humility is convenient or prudential, even if—especially if—the path leads us to our own Gethsemanes and Golgothas. This is the duty of those of us who would live the gift of Christ's meekness. Even more, it's our privilege.

Probably all of us know a living Christ in our midst, an individual who quietly and unobtrusively reflects to and for us the blessing of meekness. I'd like to close this chapter by speaking of one of them.

In the last year of his life, Henri Nouwen feverishly worked on a manuscript (which he was unable to complete before death took him) about a young man named Adam. Adam was a guest of the L'Arche Daybreak Community in Toronto, a residential community for persons with severe physical and mental handicaps. Nouwen served as chaplain at L'Arche. By all appearances, Adam was hopelessly retarded, able to communicate only through animal-like grunts and feeble, ambiguous gestures. Moreover, he was prone to terrible tremors that frequently erupted in savage epileptic seizures. There was no doubt about Adam's absolute helplessness. He required round-the-clock supervision that included a morning ritual of bathing, dressing, and feeding. Nouwen was assigned this daily two-hour task, and his unfinished book shares with us the great lesson he learned from the experience.

In the beginning of his relationship with Adam, Nouwen resented the daily regimen of caregiving. Although he tried to perform his duties with genuine solicitude, he couldn't help but feel that his energies were wasted. There were books to write, conferences to prepare, and letters to be answered. His time with Adam deflected him from his "real" ministry. Besides, the basic assistance he gave Adam could have just as easily been provided by someone else with fewer responsibilities—by someone, quite frankly, less important.

But what initially was an unwelcome burden eventually became a revelation, for in this broken and utterly impoverished youth Nouwen began to sense a hidden life of incredible richness, not in spite of but because of Adam's destitution. In Adam's quiet patience with his reluctant caregiver's often-fumbling attempts to bathe or feed him, Nouwen discerned the forbearance of God. In Adam's simple, unself-conscious acceptance of his own absolute lowliness, Nouwen recognized the unpretentious but breathtakingly dignified humility of the God who pitches his tent among us. And in Adam's uncomplicated and unashamed dependence on the strength of others, Nouwen intuited the freedom that comes from *ptoches*.

Over time, says Nouwen, Adam "in some mysterious way [became] an image of the living Christ for me..., a revelation of Christ among us....Adam did not have to practice the spiritual disciplines to become empty for God. His so-called disability gifted him with that."[19] Nouwen realized that what the Nietzschean world unhesitatingly dismisses as a particularly repellent example of ineffective, powerless "meekness" is in reality the engrafted Word. In gazing into Adam's trusting, patient, gentle, and suffering eyes, Nouwen beheld God's. "Those two [daily] hours [with Adam] were pure gift, a time of contemplation, during which we, together, were touching something of God. With Adam I knew a sacred presence and I 'saw the face of God.'"[20]

And in discovering God's face in Adam's, Nouwen experienced great healing, for Adam's meekness awakened and called forth the divine gift of meekness in Nouwen's own heart. In the young man's weakness was God's strength, and that strength patiently but inexorably beckoned to Nouwen to follow the way of gentle gratitude and humble self-forgetfulness himself.

> It was as if Adam kept pulling me back to earth, to the ground of being, to the source of life. My many words,

spoken or written, always tempted me to go up into lofty ideas and perspectives without keeping in touch with the dailiness and beauty of ordinary life. Adam didn't allow this.[21]

After Adam's death, when Nouwen sat down to try to express what the young man had meant to him, he came to the conclusion that "Adam was chosen to witness to God's love through his brokenness."[22] In writing these words, Nouwen put his finger on the heart of meekness. When we enter into a meekness that participates in Christ's own lowliness, we witness God's presence to the world, because we step out of the way and make room for God's presence in the world. Adam's example teaches us that this imitation of divine meekness is not only a great blessing for ourselves. It also, as we'll explore more fully in chapter 3, ministers to others.

CHAPTER TWO

Mercy

*We are not called to judge or to condemn but to be instruments of life,
to give life and to receive life.*

Jean Vanier

Forgotten Truths

Children have the quite wonderful talent of hearing with
undiminished interest the same story over and over again. No
matter how often a favorite tale is repeated, they listen with
eager, enthusiastic freshness. Sadly, most of us lose this ability
with the passage of time. We stimuli-hungry adults scurry around
in pursuit of the latest thrill and newest fad. For us, repetition
breeds a certain amount of jaded weariness—"been there, done
that"—which in turn closes us off to the deep meaning that may
be embedded in familiar stories.

This loss of receptivity is particularly striking when it comes to
the parables in the New Testament. We adult Christians have heard
or read them so often that our eyes tend to glaze and our thoughts
wander when we run across them yet again in a sermon or book.
We switch over to automatic pilot, as it were, mechanically coast-

ing along with the same old tired interpretations we've relied on for years. As a consequence, we no longer hear what the parables have to tell us. We're too habituated to them to pay attention to what they actually say. (I suspect, by the way, that Jesus' admonition for us to "become like little children" is in part a warning against this kind of bored deafness.)

If there was ever a parable that familiarity and repetition have deadened, it's got to be the story of the Good Samaritan. All of us, even those who haven't darkened a church door or opened a Bible in years, can recite it practically word for word. Yes, yes, we yawn. It's about being a good neighbor. The Samaritan is a better neighbor than the priest or the Levite because he pitied the man robbed on the road to Jerusalem. So may we all. Amen.

When we drag out this canned interpretation on the assumption that it exhausts the parable's meaning, we close our hearts to at least three significant points. The first is that the parable isn't actually about pity at all. The Samaritan was a good neighbor precisely because he showed *mercy*. In concluding the tale with the instruction to "go and do likewise" (Luke 10:37), Jesus is explicitly recommending mercy-giving, not pitying.

The second point is that authentic mercy, Christian mercy, is neither *just* feeling sorry for someone who's in a bad way, nor *just* tending that person's physical and psychic wounds. The priest and the Levite who averted their heads and walked on by could well have experienced distress at the sight of the broken wayfarer. Similarly, the Samaritan (even though he didn't) could have ministered to the man—dressing his wounds, getting him to a sickbed at the inn, paying for his convalescent care—out of a cold sense of duty that lacked even the slightest twinge of compassion for his plight. These very real possibilities suggest that true mercy must involve both an inner and an outer response. Sympathizing with the suffering of another won't do in the absence of concrete action. Conversely, action that's not fueled by genuine compassion is also insufficient.

The third and most important point of the parable is that Christian mercy's real aim reaches far beyond the immediate emotion of sympathy or the dressing of wounds (although these, of course, are essential). Incalculably more important is its goal of breathing life into others, of enabling them to reclaim their identity and destiny as beings made in the likeness of God. The mercy-giver, as Jean Vanier suggests in the passage quoted at the beginning of this chapter, is called to be an instrument of life, an enabler, a creator. This is the real secret of the Good-Samaritan parable: that to bestow mercy is to give life, and in giving life, to receive it.

Our forgetfulness of these three deep truths is tantamount to a kind of spiritual amnesia that blocks us from the *integritas* so important for our development as Christians. The consequence is twofold: we continue to mouth allegiance to the fifth Beatitude without appreciating what it actually entails, and in the process we gradually absorb the secular world's Nietzschean opinion that there's something suspicious about mercy-giving and mercy-receiving. This suspicion clashes with our ostensible fidelity to mercy as a spiritual value, thereby churning up the same dissonance between public profession and private belief we observed in the case of meekness. Before we quite realize what's happened, we find ourselves uncomfortably close to Nietzsche's repudiation of mercy as morally repugnant.

The initial step in curing ourselves of spiritual amnesia is to identify and face our confused notions about mercy. Since so many of them reflect to one degree or another Nietzsche's condemnation of Christian mercy, the first thing to do is gaze into the mirror he holds in front of us.

Mercy as Pity

Have you ever been uneasily suspicious that your pity for another person, regardless of your good intentions, was actually harmful, pampering him or her and burdening you? Or have you had someone nail you to the wall with a piercing scowl and the scornful parting shot of "I *pity* you!"? If so, you have distasteful, firsthand acquaintance with what Nietzsche thinks Christian mercy is really all about.

Like too many of us, Nietzsche thinks of "pity" as a synonym for "mercy." For him, mercy is nothing more than the emotional response of "feeling sorry" for the plight of another person. It's obviously possible for non-Christians to experience pity. But Christianity, according to Nietzsche, is *the* "religion of pity," placing a higher value on "feeling sorry" for others than any other faith tradition.[1] And this is precisely the problem, for nothing, insists Nietzsche, is more morally repugnant, more "unhealthy" and "mortally dangerous," than Christian pity.[2] It needlessly perpetuates misery and weakness on the one hand, and bestows the illusion of power while actually sapping strength on the other. Not that Nietzsche has anything against power. What irks him is that pity breeds a false sense of empowerment rather than the genuine article.

Let's examine both of these claims in turn.

We saw in the last chapter that Nietzsche divides humans into two mutually exclusive groups: "masters" and "slaves."

Masters are those individuals with the strength and determination to embrace their instinctual drives, run with their passions, and take themselves as the ultimate standards of value. Slaves, on the other hand, are timid, spiritless, and ineffectual herd creatures who both fear their own repressed wills to power and resentfully envy the independent stalwartness of masters.

Nietzsche clearly thinks masters are psychologically and morally superior to slaves. They're what humans *ought* to be, whereas slaves are stunted caricatures. But masters are advantaged from an evolutionary perspective as well. Their exuberant will to power and their high sense of adventure make them better able to survive and thrive in a world red in tooth and claw. Thus the blond beast, coming as he does from superior stock, can outsmart and outlast the bumbling herd creature. It's only a matter of time before the slave goes the way of the dinosaur. His meekness ultimately hamstrings him from competing in the evolutionary race for survival.

So far as Nietzsche's concerned, the extinction of the slave herd can't come too soon. But Christian pity throws a monkey wrench into the great evolutionary machine. Pity may not completely stall the motor, but it does slow it down, and Nietzsche finds this intolerable. The way in which pity disrupts the natural course of evolution is by teaching that slaves ought to be saved rather than let to die, that their wretched condition properly calls for a "feeling sorry" response rather than contemptuous indifference. In preaching pity as a supreme religious value, then, Christianity foolishly encourages the perpetuation of a type of human who contributes nothing to the race, who is a burden to himself and an embarrassment to his betters, and who by rights ought to be allowed to perish:

Pity on the whole thwarts the law of evolution, which is the law of selection. It preserves what is ripe for destruction; it defends life's disinherited and condemned; through the abundance of the ill-constituted of all kinds which it retains in life, it gives life itself a gloomy and questionable aspect.[3]

And what's the decisive factor in the evolutionary "selection" with which pity interferes? There's no surprise here: it's nothing less than the will to power, that "healthy" instinct, "bent on preserving and enhancing the value of life," which is utterly alien to the cowardly meekness of the slave.[4] In throwing up roadblocks to evolution's natural preference for the will-to-powered master, Christian pity both preserves slavish weakness and allows the contagion of meekness to infect whole new generations. Thus it is "a multiplier of misery and a conservator of everything miserable."[5] But this is sheer madness. Far better to boldly face the fact that the slave is destined for extinction, and to cooperate with the natural order of things by ruthlessly withholding pity. In the long run, this is the "kindest"—and certainly the "healthiest"—thing to do. "To be physician *here*, to be inexorable *here*, to wield the knife *here*—that pertains to *us* [that is, to masters], that is *our* kind of philanthropy."[6]

So much for Nietzsche's first reason for blasting Christian mercy as morally repugnant. What about his second: that mercy breeds a perniciously false sense of empowerment?

Although inescapably destined for extinction, slaves—like all life forms, even lower ones—desperately wish to survive. So they adopt hit-or-miss strategies that sustain, at least for the short run, their physical continuation and psychological balance. These strategies are substitutes for iron-willed power, since the slave by definition has none. They're the same kind of underhanded ruses employed by any inferior species unable to defend itself in an honest and straightforward fashion.

We've already examined one of these subterfuges: the rationalization of meekness, whereby the slave tries to compensate for his own miserable weakness by transvaluing it from vice to Christian virtue. In making this move, the slave simultaneously gives himself the illusion of spiritual purity and demonizes the master by condemning his genuine superiority as a spiritual flaw. Of course, argues Nietzsche, this is simply an attempt at one-upmanship, the desperately envious struggle of a weakling to transform bitter necessity into virtue. But for all its self-deception, the strategy gives the slave something to hold onto. It grants him a sense (albeit a false one) of power, and if he's extremely lucky, his constant holier-than-thou jeremiads against the will to power just might chip away at some of the master's self-confidence. Even a blond beast isn't completely immune to the incessant yipping of mongrels who wish to bring him down to their level.

The ruse of Christian mercy operates along analogous lines. The slave realizes that his innate timidity so weakens him that he requires the pity of others simply to survive. But he can't abide the shame of cravenly depending on the largesse of others, so he transvalues pity into a moral duty. Now any mercy shown him isn't merely a bone thrown to a dog. It becomes something to which he has a *right—a God-given* right—and this disguises, at least in his own mind, the odiousness of his condition.

The transvaluation of pity into Christian duty empowers the slave in two insidious ways. In the first place, his self-righteous demand for pity begins to sap the master's energetic strength. Confronted on all sides by miserable creatures who clamor for his physical and emotional solicitude, the master is deflected from his course of rugged self-determination. As Nietzsche has already pointed out, pity is a "multiplier of misery." In taking the moral high ground that the master owes him pity, the slave in effect tries to force the master to shoulder him as a burden. There is "a secret seduction in all this," says Nietzsche. "How is it possible to stay on one's *own* path? Always someone crying calls us aside; our eye rarely sees a case where it does not become necessary to leave our own task immediately," and dissipate valuable energy and resources in pity.[7] By sucking the master into his own orbit of petty misery, the slave strengthens his own position and diminishes the master's.

But the slave isn't content with stopping here. It's not enough for him merely to assert his strength by weakening the master; he secretly longs to be a master himself. So the second way in which the transvaluation of pity into moral duty consolidates the illusion of power is by making the slave feel superior when he himself grants pity to another. Nietzsche points out that there's a hidden perversity to pity. We do not admire or respect those for whom we "feel sorry."[8] Instead, we look upon them with a certain amount of disdain: they're pitiful precisely because they're too ineffectually weak to make it on their own. So in exercising the "virtue" of pity, the slave can at one and the same time congratulate himself on his fidelity to Christian duty and assume a position of condescending superiority to the object of his pity. Moreover, his bestowal of pity places the person who's pitied in his control. To take pity on someone is to grant them a boon they don't really deserve, and this means they incur a debt that can never be paid off.

Obviously this is all highly irrational. On the one hand, the slave whiningly displays his own weakness in order to gain pity from the master; on the other hand, he wields pity as a weapon by which to subjugate others and strut as a master himself. But then the trademark of most defense mechanisms *is* irrationality. The slave isn't concerned with consistency. His only urge is to survive, using whatever resources are available to him. Given his essential weakness, those resources are limited to rationalization, manipulation, and the delusional pretense of Christian "purity." But each of these, when viewed from an objective, non-Christian position, must be condemned as repellent. Little wonder that a true master views all this with distaste and concludes that "my humanity does not consist in pitying men but in *enduring* my pity for them."[9]

Cheap Mercy

Our reaction to Nietzsche's savaging of Christian mercy is probably very much like our earlier one to his assault against Christian meekness: dazed shock and angry denial. He's got everything backwards! He's again twisting everything around to suit his own purposes!

I agree in the main with this response. But as was the case with Nietzsche's criticism of meekness, I think his equally acerbic challenge to mercy deserves to be taken seriously. Honest self-examination disclosed that many of us buy, to one degree or another, the Nietzschean disdain for meekness, despite the fact that we continue to pay it religious lip service. Honesty again forces us to admit that many of us likewise subtly sympathize at a deep level with Nietzsche's condemnation of mercy, even though we publicly profess allegiance to it.

Most of our difficulties arise because we, like Nietzsche, insist on identifying Christian mercy with pity. This is an understandable confusion; as we'll see shortly, pity bears at least a sur-face similarity to mercy. But pity, especially as Nietzsche uses the term, is not the same as mercy. Indeed, it's a low-budget imitation that's antithetical to a genuinely merciful spirit.

The theologian and martyr Dietrich Bonhoeffer coined the term "cheap grace." "Cheap grace" refers to the comfortable cer-tainty that true Christian discipleship is easily affordable, costing very little energy or sacrifice. We purchase the grace of God cheaply by going through the motions of discipleship without investing anything substantial. More or less regular church atten-dance, more or less observance of days of obligation, more or less outward conformity to the Ten Commandments and the Beatitudes: this is enough to get us by. So long as we shell out the minimally acceptable price of salvation, we stay ahead of our membership dues to the heavenly country club.[10]

Now, pity is "cheap mercy." It costs the practitioner very lit-tle—nothing, really—and the dividends are twofold: an immedi-ately satisfying feeling of doing good and the smug confidence that pity fulfills one's Christian duty to act mercifully, thus pay-ing off big time in the long run as well.

Pity is cheap mercy for three reasons. In the first place, it requires no actual interaction—or even contact—with the person whom we pity. It's a detached, aloof response to the pain of other individuals that calls for no personal involvement, much less commitment, on our parts. We needn't engage with their suffer-ing. Instead, we safely intellectualize our response to their condi-tion by evoking one abstract ethical formula or another: "People oughtn't to go hungry in a country as rich as this," for example, or "Folks who can't help themselves deserve a helping hand from those more fortunate." In making this move, we reduce a tangibly suffering person to an anonymous statistic to be plugged into a pet philosophical or public policy framework, and focus on that framework's abstract principles instead of the flesh-and-blood misery in front of us. When we "respond" by writing out a check to our favorite charity or voting for the latest "reform" candidate, we're responding not to the suffering person, but to the principle. The check or vote is cheap mercy. It salves our conscience while at the same time keeps us cleanly distanced.

The aloof impersonality characteristic of pity doesn't necessarily mean that it evokes no emotions in us. After all, most of us, like Nietzsche, tend to identify pity with "feeling sorry." But the emotions that accompany pity typically aren't at all directed to their proper object—the suffering person—but rather to ourselves. We walk down a crowded city sidewalk and spy a street person huddled against a wall, his hand out. We feel horror, or at least uneasiness, and we "take pity" on him by tossing a buck in his direction. But the horror or uneasiness we experience isn't because of *his* miserable condition. He's just a sign that occasions the chilling reminder that one day we, too, could end up on a sidewalk grate. In pitying him, then, what we're really doing is expressing anxiety about our *own* situation. The pittance we throw his way is actually tossed to ourselves. If asked why we pity him, we're quite likely to give the game away by saying: "Because I hope someone would do the same for me if I were in his shoes." Cheap mercy, again. We're not spending in the service of another; we're investing in ourselves by invoking a little karma-magic. What goes around comes around.

The second reason pity is cheap mercy is that it's thoroughly judgmental. Nietzsche is quite correct: we don't pity people we admire or consider our peers. Instead, we pity those whom we judge inferior to ourselves, and this means that there's always a condescending presumption of superiority on the part of the pity-giver. This quickly divides people into two categories: those who have failed in the great game of life, who don't have the wherewithal to make something of themselves—who are ineffectually "meek"—and those who have risen to the top through hard work and talent—the "empowered." The former are subordinate objects of pity, the latter superior pity-bestowers.

Nor does the judgmentalism of pity stop here. For within the great unwashed mass of subordinates, the pity-giver judges some to be more worthy of pity than others. The panhandler who's on the streets as a victim of industrial downsizing is more deserving of pity than the homeless drunkard. Both are unsavory, but one is a more proper recipient of our largesse than the other. "Don't waste your pity on that sot!" we warn people. "He isn't worth it!" This doesn't mean, of course, that we'll invite the unemployed person home with us until he or she finds a job. Pity, after all, remains distantly abstract. But it does mean that for "pity's sake" we'll take the time to stoop down and hand out a dollar. Cheap mercy.

There's yet another reason why pity is cheap mercy: it always expects something in return, a payoff, a compensation. We've already seen a couple of ways in which the pity-giver expects dividends: immediate psychological satisfaction from doing good, and expectations of a future reward from either karma-magic or God. But the pity-giver also expects—in fact, demands—something else as well: obsequious gratitude from the recipient of his or her pity. This only makes sense. Subordinates, even those deemed "deserving," ought to know their place and be properly thankful for help from their betters. When the gratitude the pity-giver sees as his right isn't instantly and profusely forthcoming, he's self-righteously miffed. "So *this* is the thanks I get for going out of my way to be a nice guy!"

Pity rather than genuine Christian mercy is the norm in secular society. It's what we've come to expect, and many of us also think it entirely appropriate. But we rarely speak its true nature in the bluntly harsh language of a Nietzsche. Instead, we soften its callousness by translating it into the milder discourse of psychology and public policy.

If called on for our failure (or, better, our refusal) to engage personally with the recipients of our pity, we excuse ourselves on the psychological grounds that we can only spread ourselves so thin, that we're no good to anyone if we burn out. Similarly, we try to justify the utterly selfish emotions pity stirs up by appealing to "enlightened" self-interest. "Of course the sight of a street bum upsets me," we say. "I've got to look out for Number One, don't I? I'm not a saint, you know. Better to show pity out of self-concern than not at all!" Or, switching from psychobabble to the rhetoric of sociology, we argue that the suffering caused by poverty, unemployment, racism, and so on, is "institutional" in nature, and hence, properly ought be addressed at the public policy level. Individual acts of compassion only muddy the waters. What's needed is a clear head and a certain amount of "objective" distance.

We justify our conviction that some people are more deserving of pity than others by appealing, sometimes explicitly but usually only indirectly, to one form or another of "social evolutionism," the intellectually disreputable but nonetheless popular theory that a process of selection weeds out undesirable individuals in society just as it kills off unadaptable species in nature. Life in the fast-paced world is a brutal testing ground, and only the "fittest" can survive.

It's but a short step from this to the Nietzschean conviction that only the "fittest" *ought* to survive, and that those persons (meek ones, for example) who fail the test should be allowed to fall through the cracks—for the "good" of society, you understand. Otherwise, they're simply too much of a drain on limited economic resources. To pamper and coddle them out of misguided pity only perpetuates their miserably marginal existence and needlessly burdens the rest of us. Far better to invest energy and time in those who "deserve" it—that is, in those who, in our judgment, can "contribute" or "give something back" to society.[11]

Moreover, those fortunates whom we do deem worthy of pity properly ought to feel gratitude for our aid. They should humbly recognize their lowly position in the pecking order, and thank their lucky stars that society offers them a safety net and a second chance. Nothing enrages a secular pity-giver more, for example, than a social-welfare recipient's ungrateful conviction that he or she is somehow "entitled" to public "handouts." Welfare recipients are "entitled" to nothing, and consequently, have no right either to high-handedly demand help or to withhold thanks once it's given them. "That's the problem with too many people on the welfare rolls," we disgustedly mutter. "They think they're *owed* something!"

These Nietzschean attitudes toward pity are so widespread in today's society that they've acquired the status of folk wisdom. One runs across them in newspaper editorials and letters, radio talk shows, political debates, coffeehouse bull sessions, college essays. And yet they're by no means confined to the secular sphere, are they? They slide over into the religious arena as well.

It's difficult to compartmentalize deep-seated convictions. Secular sensibilities flood into the Christian pew and pulpit, with the result that the old dissonance between public profession and private belief once more wells up.

We Christians all know that the fifth Beatitude prescribes mercy as an integral part of the spiritual life. We're also well familiar with scripture's teaching that mercy, like rain, ought to fall down indiscriminately, that it should be sown profligately, that it demands the personal commitment and hands-on engagement of a Good Samaritan, and that, like the prodigal son's father, we should be joyfully grateful for the opportunity of bestowing it, neither expecting nor desiring anything for ourselves in return. Yet too often our unarticulated Nietzschean identification of mercy with pity deafens us to these truths, and we take the easy out and bestow cheap, rather than authentically Christian, mercy.

One way in which the disparity between what we Christians profess and what we really believe comes across in a slight-of-hand the Anglican theologian J. B. Phillips calls "imitation" spirituality. We mimic or ape true spirituality, going through the motions of devotion, prayer, confession, compassion, and love out of a burdensome sense of duty rather than any genuine conviction. As Phillips insightfully notes, "It is perfectly possible for us to behave kindly, justly, and correctly toward one another and yet withhold [a] giving of the 'self.'"[12]

The withholding of self that Phillips singles out as the central characteristic of imitation spirituality is likewise the defining quality of the cheap mercy practiced by many Christians. Instead of intimately engaging—heart and soul—with the lives of suffering persons, we merely *act* engaged. Instead of focusing on humans, we fixate on an abstract concept of Christian duty. Or, even worse, we withhold our self out of the misguided assumption that our only real allegiance as Christians is to God. Getting entangled in the messy suffering of others deflects us from the true purpose of our existence. Besides, the best way to show mercy is through prayerful intercession, not hands-on involvement.

Nor are we Christians immune from the insidious *judgmentalism* of pity, even though scripture tells us time and again that God alone has the right to judge. This judgmentalism typically expresses itself, as Thomas Merton points out, in what can only be described as pharisaic legalism: we classify, categorize, and define persons as worthy or unworthy of solicitude according to how well they live up to our "Christian" standards.

Merton reminds us that Jesus told the parable of the Good Samaritan in response to the lawyer's question, "If I'm to love my neighbor, who is my neighbor?" The lawyer operated from the assumption that "some men are better than others." So, "in order to protect himself against loving an unworthy object and thus wasting his love, he wanted to know where to draw the line....The question is a matter of classification. Therefore it is a matter of judgment also, for to classify is to judge."[13] But there's something intrinsically broken about this division of people into neighbor and non-neighbor, elect and damned, sheep and goats.

> If a man has to be pleasing to me, comforting, reassuring, before I can love him, then I cannot truly love him. Not that love cannot console or reassure! But if I demand first to be reassured, I will never dare to love. If a man has to be a Jew or a Christian before I can love him, then I cannot love him. If he has to be black or white before I can love him, then I cannot love him. If he has to belong to

my political party or social group before I can love him, if he has to wear my kind of uniform, then my love is no longer love: it is dictated by something outside myself....I love not the person but his classification, and in that event I love him not as a person but as a thing. I love his label...[14]

The consequence of a pseudo-Christian mercy that presumes to judge worth or unworth is the acceptance of what might be called "supernatural selection," a religious analogue to social and natural selection. The reformer Martin Luther nicely captures the essence of supernatural selection:

> [I]t cannot have pity or mercy for the frail and weak, but insists on the strictest enforcement and the purest selection; as soon as there is even a minor flaw, all mercy is gone, and there is nothing but fuming and fury....True holiness is merciful and sympathetic, but all that false holiness can do is to rage and fume.[15]

The fuming and fury Luther alludes to in this passage clearly suggest a lack of both patience and empathy for the perceived spiritual weaknesses of others. But such intolerance only makes sense if we've already written such persons off as hopelessly degenerate cases unable to cut it on the demanding obstacle course of Christian righteousness. Naturally, opinion as to what counts as unsalvageable corruption will differ. Catholics, Protestants, non-Christians, erring members of one's own congregation: each is a candidate for someone's list of properly endangered religious species. Once pity is confused with genuine mercy, anyone is fair game—except, of course, the pity-giver. He or she is religiously superior, tried and proven in the great contest of spiritual selection.

Finally, we Christians tend to be just as resentful as secularists when we feel that our condescending solicitude hasn't been accepted with the gratitude it deserves. How could we not? Cheap mercy always operates from the assumption that the pity-giver is superior to the pity-recipient, and this necessarily means that the latter is indebted to the former. Since the pity-recipient has neither the spiritual nor material wherewithal to ever repay the debt, the least he or she can do is show effusive thanks, and if she doesn't, we feel slighted.

Let me illustrate this with an experience of my own, one that still reddens me with shame whenever I recall it. My guess is that many Christians could tell similar stories.

As a college student, I put in a lot of time at the local food bank and soup kitchen. I fancied myself a genuine (but appropriately modest) saint who walked the extra mile by lovingly tending to my "less fortunate" brothers and sisters. Now I realize that I gave very little but expected a great deal in return. Cheap mercy.

The moment of truth arrived for me one Thanksgiving. I'd volunteered to "sacrifice" my holiday by working the kitchen and soup line. I tied on a newly starched apron that was as stiff and unnatural as the piously pitying face I presented to each of the homeless people who came to the shelter for a hot meal. I served up dollops of mashed potatoes and turkey as a priest hands out the sacred wafer. Most of the folks politely thanked me as I filled their plates, and I accepted their gratitude as my rightful due.

But one fellow—a particularly down-and-out man named Roscoe, who had a reputation for drug and alcohol abuse—refused to play the game. He stared at me with sour bitterness as

I served his food. When I finished loading his plate, I looked at him expectantly, offering him the opportunity to do the decent thing and express his gratitude. Roscoe obviously knew what was going on, and he shook with fury at my condescension. He picked up his tray, nailed me with a look of pure hatred, and softly but unmistakably said: "F—— you, college boy!"

My reaction was shock, quickly followed by seething rage. "What a *jerk*! I treat him like a human being, and this is my reward!"

It took years before I realized that instead of getting self-righteous, I should have gone over to Roscoe's table and begged his forgiveness. He had just cause to be furious. Here was a middle-class white kid, who'd really never wanted for anything in his life, playing Mother Teresa by deigning to come down to the level of the world's Roscoes in order to throw them a few crumbs of cheap mercy—and expecting, on top of everything else, to be thanked for his insufferable condescension. That kid sincerely thought he was performing a genuine work of mercy—feeding the hungry. But what he was really doing was treating Roscoe (as well as the other, more polite guests of the soup kitchen) as an inferior throwback. I'd labeled Roscoe as a thing to be pitied, I'd withheld an authentically Christian giving of myself by hiding behind a goofy mask of unctuous concern, and then I had arrogantly demanded to be thanked for my few pains—all in the name of "Christian" mercy.

Mercy as Midwifery

If we're to escape the troublesome conflation of pity and mercy many of us implicitly endorse, we must rediscover the deep meaning of Christian mercy. The first step is to take a close look at the scriptural understanding of it.

In the ancient non-Christian Greek world, mercy was understood as a *pathos*: a feeling or emotion aroused by the suffering of another. As the word *pathos* suggests, mercy was seen as a response over which we have little control; it's a sentiment that overtakes us, and we're powerless (or "passive") to resist it. It comes as no surprise that skill in evoking the *pathos* of mercy in others was considered a vitally practical part of a young person's education. Athenian society was nearly as litigious as our own, and it was in a person's best interests to learn rhetorical flourishes that aroused the sympathy of a judge or jury. Emotional oratory, then as now, is extremely persuasive.

This made mercy immediately suspect to those Greek philosophers who above all valued rational self-control. The Stoics, for example, rejected appeals for mercy as unworthy strategies of manipulation, and frowned upon susceptibility to such appeals as weak emotionalism. In either case, the *pathos* of mercy interfered with the coolly detached objectivity necessary for sound judgment. Nietzsche, trained in classical philology, was well aware of both these Stoic criticisms of mercy, and echoes of them clearly sound throughout his condemnation of Christian "pity."

What Nietzsche overlooked (or perhaps chose to ignore) is that the Greek understanding of mercy as primarily a passive emotional response is not at all what ancient Hebrew and Christian authors meant when *they* used the word. Mercy in both the Old Testament (*chesed*) and the New (*eleos*) is not a feeling so much as a way of being, one of benevolent loving-kindness that has as its sole purpose the awakening of its recipients to new life.

Mercy is an attitude and comportment that creatively reflects the loving-kindness of the God who birthed all creation in the first place. By acting mercifully, we participate in and continue the ongoing mystery of divine gestation. We become spiritual mid-wives—midwives in the service of God.

Thomas Merton correctly reminds us that the abiding characteristic assigned to God throughout all scripture is mercy, that "brass bell and undersong of the whole Bible."[16] The book of Exodus first sounds the bell by describing Yahweh as a God of *chesed*: "The LORD, the LORD, a God merciful and gracious, slow to anger, and abounding in steadfast love and faithfulness, keeping steadfast love for thousands" (Exod 34:6). The Psalmist takes up the refrain: "O LORD..., thy steadfast love is good; according to thy abundant mercy, turn to me" (Ps 69:16); "Bless the LORD, O my soul..., who crowns you with steadfast love and mercy" (Ps 103:1, 4); "Great is thy mercy, O LORD" (Ps 119:156).

The prophets, for all their dire warnings of divine retribution for the wicked, similarly insist that mercy is the primary quality of God. Yahweh assures the people through Isaiah that he will gather and replenish them with "great mercies," showering the "everlasting love" of "mercy" upon them (Isa 54:6, 8). Even when God is wrathful over Israel's iniquities, Jeremiah reassures his listeners that the divine essence is "steadfast love and mercy" (Jer 16:5). Daniel also comforts frightened sinners by promising them that God's might is forever tempered with mercy (Dan 2:18–23), and that this mercy is utterly reliable (Dan 9:18).

Divine mercy or *eleos* is also the central theme ringing throughout the New Testament. "The Lord's mercy is trustworthy," says Paul (1 Cor 7:25), manifesting itself from the unexpected quickening of a child in the aged Elizabeth (Luke 1:58) to the gift, "rich in mercy" (Eph 2:4), of the Incarnation, to the aton-ing event of Christ's passion, death, and resurrection. But the New Testament makes explicit what the Old merely hinted at: that the mercy of God is a mysterious fecundity that grants us a second birth, a fresh start. Just as Paul was reborn through divine mercy on the Damascus Road, so that same mercy rebirths each of us. The apostle Peter repeats this claim in a scriptural text that's second in importance only to the fifth Beatitude: "By his great mercy we have been born anew" (1 Pet 1:3).

What does it mean to be "born anew" by God's mercy? Perhaps the best way to understand it is to think of a conversion experience. In both Hebrew (*teshuba*) and Greek (*metanoia*), "con-version" literally means a "turning around" or a "return." We are breathed into being by the loving-kindness of divine mercy and, even more, graced with a likeness to the God who enables our existence. As a consequence, we not only partake of the divine quality of loving-kindness. We also, because of that participation, enjoy an original unity of heart and mind with God. But our sense of oneness frequently crumbles as we progress through life. The beast of self-will asserts itself, and the unity established by loving-kindness erodes. When this happens, we swerve from our destined paths toward *makarios*, toward full being, and begin instead the sorry descent toward that desolate nothingness that characterizes the state of separation from God. The covenant between God and the children of Abraham—and we are all children of Abraham—is nothing less than the promise of this original oneness. When the covenant is broken, the oneness is ruptured.

But because God is above all a God of *eleos*, he refuses to sit by as we fall from deep to deeper. The loving-kindness that enabled our existence in the first place is eternally given, ceaselessly exert-

ing itself to draw us back into the covenant so that the original
unity may be reestablished and our true identities as creatures
made in the divine likeness may be rediscovered. God's first and
unfailing love for us (1 John 4:19) continuously pulsates, coaxing
us away from the slide into nothingness, drawing us back into the
fold of being, nudging us in the direction of a metanoiac turn-
about. Sometimes the return is dramatically instantaneous: Paul's
teshuba on the Damascus Road is a case in point. But usually it's
gradual and cumulative, beset with temporary setbacks—such as
those endured by the Hebrews during their wilderness sojourn—
that are fueled by our own obstinacy and self-assertiveness.

Divine mercy, then, is a great spiritual magnet that seeks to
patiently draw us away from our wayward embrace of nothingness
back toward our true identities as creatures who partake in God's
being. "In him we live and move and have our being" (Acts 17:28).
This return, or course, is the new birth, the fresh start, the recovery of oneness. But the magnet's force of attraction is loving-kindness, and love never seeks to coerce. Instead, it enables. Love
makes itself available at all times, extends the invitation to being,
and in doing so labors to awaken us to the folly of our actions.
Love assures its recipients that all they need do to turn the corner
is open themselves to the pull of being. Love promises that it will
abide, encouraging and aiding them for as long as it takes. Love,
the patient and self-giving love of divine mercy, is a steadfast midwife who never leaves our side so long as a new birth is possible.
And given our likeness to God, rebirth is *always* possible.

Those who have been quickened and "born anew" by the *eleos*
of God are called to be incarnations of the mercy graciously
bestowed on them. Thus mercy, like meekness, is a spiritual gift,
a "wisdom from above" (Jas 3:17) intended to be passed on to

others so that the original oneness between God and humans may be reestablished for all. This obligation comes through clearly in both the Old and New Testaments. In Zechariah, the "word of the Lord" is that we "show mercy and kindness each to his brother" in imitation of the *chesed* shown us by God (Zech 7:9). Hosea, in recording God's love poem to humankind, says the only sacrifice God desires from us is mercy to others (Hos 6:6), and the evangelist Matthew twice repeats this same message for the benefit of the early Christians (Matt 9:13, 12:7).

Jesus also urges his followers to be merciful *(eleemon)* in imitation of divine mercy *(eleos)*, and not just in the Sermon on the Mount. In the parable of the steward who refuses to forgive the debts of his subordinates even though his own debts have been forgiven by the king (or God), Jesus has the king pointedly ask: "Should you not have had mercy on your fellow servant, as I had mercy on you?" (Matt 18:33). Similarly, as I pointed out at the start of this chapter, Jesus' story of the Good Samaritan has mercy as its main lesson: the parable's hero is the man who "showed *eleos*" to the distressed traveler (Luke 10:37). One of Jesus' primary criticisms of the Pharisees is that their lockstep fidelity to the law caused them to neglect "the weightier matter" of mercy (Matt 23:23), and Jesus himself doesn't hesitate to stretch the law for the sake of merciful action (e.g., Matt 9:10, 12:2; Mark 2:16, 2:24, 7:2; Luke 5:30, 5:33, 7:39; John 5:10, 6:52). The apostle James later repeats the point: "Mercy triumphs over judgment" (Jas 2:13), echoing Hosea's insistence that mercy is more worthy than even the most scrupulous conformity to religious convention.

The notion of mercy that comes through if we read scripture carefully is as different from Nietzschean pity as it can be. God's mercy is an act of loving-kindness, freely given even to the point of self-sacrifice, entirely without expectation of recompense, that bestows on us the grace of spiritual quickening. As Jesus told Nicodemus (John 3), it sweeps away the old self and enables the emergence of a new one radiant with the gift of loving-kindness and eager to pass it on to others so that they, too, might be renewed. This mercy that God bestows and that we're called to imitate is an invitation directed to each of us as concretely situated persons. It doesn't make judgments about worth, but gives itself equally to all; views its recipients as particular individuals rather than abstract statistical integers; commits itself to us in hands-on engagement, rather than distancing itself from us for the sake of "objectivity"; and has as its sole purpose the loving enablement of broken men and women toward a richer existence. *Chesed, eleos,* mercy: This is the gift of being, conveyed to us by the God who loved us into existence and faithfully continues to love us toward fulfillment. As Peter said, we are born again in and through and by God's great mercy. And that mercy has nothing to do with a pity that manipulates for its own gain on the one hand or condescendingly throws a few crumbs of cheap consolation on the other.

Living Mercifully

We've seen that mercy is essentially a spiritual enablement: God bestows the loving-kindness of *chesed* or *eleos* on us to aid us in recovering the full being of original oneness. We also saw that scripture enjoins us to live the gift of mercy by comporting ourselves in the world with such loving-kindness to our fellows that we cooperate in the enablement of their new birth. But how do we go about this? How, in practical terms, do we live mercifully?

There are three related steps to living and passing on the gift of mercy: recognizing the personhood of each and every human we meet; feeling compassion for the suffering that prevents others from realizing their own personhood, suffering that retards their rediscovery of the *makarios* offered by God; and taking concrete steps, even to the point of self-sacrifice, to help them come into the promised new birth. To flesh out mercy's three steps of recognition, compassion, and action, we may once again turn to the parable of the Good Samaritan.

Recognition

Jesus tells us that first a priest and then a Levite passed by the robbed and beaten man on the Jericho-Jerusalem road. Both of them saw the stricken man, and both of them went out of their way—detouring to the other side of the road—to avoid contact with him. We don't know if the man was unconscious or if he called out for help. But the story leaves no doubt about two things: he was in need, and the priest and the Levite were aware of that need.

Heartless as their behavior was, it's difficult to imagine that the sight of the beaten wayfarer failed to evoke pity in the priest and Levite. All we need do to appreciate this likelihood is recall the times we've acted similarly. Perhaps we've run across a homeless person as he shivered on a heating grate, or a psychotic street person ranting and raving as she and her shopping cart barreled down the sidewalk toward us. Chances are good that we, like the priest and Levite, went out of our way to avoid eye contact with these unfortunates. That, after all, seems to be the prudential rule of thumb that's as operative today as it was in ancient Israel.

Never look a bum or a crazy in the eye; they'll misinterpret it as an invitation. But chances are also good that even as we made a wide angle around them, we pitied their condition. "God!" we muttered. "How awful! How could anyone live like that?" Nonetheless, we passed them by.

How is this possible? How can we pity the suffering of another, yet do nothing to alleviate it? The problem is that pity observes the signs of suffering, but fails to recognize the *person* behind the suffering. Pity focuses on the frighteningly obvious misery of hopeless pain, but ignores the human face on which it rides. So, in a move characteristic of cheap mercy, pity distances itself from personal involvement with the victim by objectifying him or her into an abstract casualty. The priest and the Levite pityingly shake their heads when they see the man at the side of the road: the authorities simply *must* do something about brigands in this part of the country! Similarly, we pityingly observe the suffering of a homeless person, and immediately read it as yet another statistical confirmation of the need for better social services. But when suffering is intellectualized in this way, the concrete gets drowned in the abstract, and the person actually enduring pain falls through the cracks. He or she is reduced to nothing more than a symbol of something radically wrong with the system and becomes, in the most literal sense of the word, an "object" of pity—that is, a thing.

The American philosopher William James nailed this objectification of persons on the head when he called it the "sentimentalist fallacy." According to James, this fallacy consists in professing loving concern for the welfare of abstract "humanity," while all the time aloofly disregarding the well-being of individual humans. Sentimentalists never open themselves to actual persons, because their fixation on abstract models of social reform or ethical theories reduces such persons to the status of data— things to be labeled, categorized, and plugged into the latest intellectual paradigm. So even as the sentimentalist gushes over the need to champion "human" rights or work for the betterment of suffering "humankind," he or she crosses the street to avoid personal entanglement with the very persons whose suffering she abstractly "pities." In doing so, she reduces them to nonhuman objects—and obviously protects herself from the unpleasant task of actually dirtying her hands by doing something for them.[17] (Something like this, by the way, was what I did so many Thanksgivings ago to Roscoe and his fellow guests at the soup kitchen.) But the person who practices genuine mercy instead of the cheap substitute of pity isn't blinded in this way. His or her primary concern isn't an abstract concept of humanity, but rather a concretely situated individual.

As St. Paul wisely observed, the merciful Christian is simply incapable even of regarding anyone from a merely "human" point of view (2 Cor 5:16). This is because the gift of loving-kindness graciously bestowed on him or her by God awakens him to a recognition of his own concrete personhood, and in the process allows him to recognize it in others as well. He knows himself to be essentially lovable, despite all his fragile shortcomings and distasteful failures, because he's made in the image of a loving God, and he recognizes that this same blessing extends to all. He realizes that his own Godlikeness makes him a *subject* irrevocably linked to the divine Subject, a *person* akin to the supreme Personhood of God, and that all humans are given this identical gift. He humbly understands that God's loyal and loving recognition of him as a person is the mercy that prevents him from hurtling headlong into the nothingness of anonymous thinghood, and he gratefully accepts the obligation and privilege of aiding God to prevent others from falling into the same abyss. He knows that his ultimate fulfillment depends on a rebirthing embrace of his true identity as a being at-oned with God, and he wishes with all his heart to enable others to experience this new birth as well.

So the person of genuine Christian mercy reaches beyond a surface pity that distances him or her from others, and thus, recognizes them as the persons they are. And in this act of recognition, he or she reaffirms a oneness with both them and the God of mercy whose loving enablement offers the gift of being to all, millionaire or street person, Samaritan or Jew, priest or Levite. Merciful recognition, then, is not simply the first step toward mending the ruptured relationship between God and persons. It also begins to reestablish the original intimacy between us and our brothers and sisters.

The psychologist Robert Coles tells a story about Dorothy Day, cofounder of the Catholic Workers movement, that beautifully illustrates the gift of recognition granted to a person of authentic mercy. While a student at Columbia Medical School, Coles found himself increasingly moved by Dorothy's writings and life. So one day he decided to hop a subway to the Catholic Worker house where she lived and worked and introduce himself. When Coles arrived at the house, Dorothy was seated at a table talking with a young woman. One of the Catholic Workers told Dorothy that a young man had come to call. Dorothy glanced at Coles, motioned for him to wait, and turned back to her table companion.

Coles immediately sized up the woman at the table with Dorothy as a street person. Her face and clothes were dirty, her

hair unkempt, her shoes ragged. She was agitated, almost hysterical, and Coles the medical student suspected she was either an
addict badly in need of a fix or a psychotic. Time and again the
wild-eyed woman seemed on the edge of exploding, and each
time Dorothy soothingly stroked her hand or murmured a few
words of comfort. Coles was amazed at her patience.

At last the woman simmered down long enough for Dorothy
to walk over to Coles. Her greeting stunned him. "I understand
you've been waiting," she said. "I'm sorry we've kept you so long.
Which of us did you want to speak to?"[18]

Coles never forgot Dorothy's words, and neither should we.
For they reflect the deep recognition of personhood that comes
from genuine mercy. Here was Dorothy Day, an internationally
famous woman, who saw so little distinction between herself and
a hysterical street woman that it never occurred to her that Coles
had come down to the Bowery only to make her acquaintance.
This wasn't false modesty on Dorothy's part, but rather an expectation that the Godlike person behind the young woman's suffering whom she recognized and loved was equally recognized and
loved by others as well. An unlikely possibility, perhaps, as the
parable of the Good Samaritan reminds us, though the unlikeli-
ness of it ought not to be.

This same recognition is what distinguishes the Good
Samaritan from the priest and the Levite. They pity, but he is
merciful. His mercy allows him to see what the priest and the
Levite can't or won't: that the body sprawled broken and bleed-
ing at the side of the road is a person—precious, like himself, in
the eyes of God. In mercifully responding to the robbed man, the
Good Samaritan didn't just see him as an impersonal statistic to

be plugged into a conceptual grid. He recognized him as a mysterious extension of both God and himself.

Compassion

Recognition prepares the way for mercy's second stage, compassion. Unlike pity, compassion is a genuinely engaged response to another human being's plight. When we experience it, we don't merely feel detached concern about a breakdown in the system, much less a self-referential anxiety that the suffering we observe might one day come to smite *us*. Instead, our recognition of the personhood we share with the victim necessarily means that we also share his pain. Because of the deep bond that links his being with ours, we feel it as he does, endure his burden as our burden, too. We relate to him with our entire self, not just our intellect.

The New Testament authors were well aware of both the spiritual depth and intensity of this mode of relating. The word they used when writing of compassion was *splangchnizomai*. It's startlingly evocative. *Splangchna* are entrails, guts, bowels. To be moved by compassion is to be affected and afflicted at one's deepest core. It's a gut-wrenching sharing of someone else's pain.

Obviously, connecting compassionately with another's pain is a disruptive experience, and many of us fearfully barricade ourselves against the possibility of such an onslaught. As should be clear by now, one of the more predictable defense strategies is to practice the cheap mercy of pity. Transforming the victim into an object avoids the unpleasant possibility of recognizing him as a person, and consequently, of enduring *splangchnizomai*. After all, how can one empathize with a mere thing? The priest and the Levite both safeguard against an empathic seizure of the guts by doing precisely this. They close themselves off to the stricken man's personhood, and hence sever the connection between him and them that makes true compassion possible. Had they actually taken the time to help the stricken man, the most they would have done is impatiently given him a mouthful of water or a couple words of formulaic comfort. Or they might have written a letter to the newspaper, calling for more conscientious policing of the Jericho-Jerusalem road. And this would have been more than enough for them to walk away with clean hands. What else can one be expected to do for a mere object?

But Jesus tells us that the Samaritan saw the man, recognized him for the subject he was, and "had compassion" for him. Even though he left the wounded man for a few days in the care of an innkeeper, we can be sure that the Samaritan carried the burden of the victim's wounds with him all the way to Jerusalem and back. The compassion born from mercy had made the wounds his own, burying them deeply in his bowels.

To share another person's pain as the Good Samaritan did, we must relinquish, at least for the moment, our own insulated interests and all-too-human preoccupation with self. There simply isn't enough room inside us for both our own ego-needs and the needs of another. When the gut-wrenching experience of compassion overtakes us, the priority of the other's interests over our own is clear, and we willingly self-empty in the other's service. Henri Nouwen calls this "voluntary displacement," a sacrifice of self that "moves us from positions of distinction to positions of sameness," from enclosed individualism and distinctiveness to empathic union. "To disappear...as an object of [self-]interest" for the sake of someone else is not only the essence of compassion.

It's also "the basic move of the Christian life," imitating as it does the mystery of God's self-emptying in the Incarnation.[19]

The empathic union that occurs when compassion moves us to voluntarily displace our own interests obviously doesn't accommodate the judgmentalism by which pity makes its distinctions between deserving sheep and undeserving goats. Judgmentalism is only possible when I invoke myself as the standard by which to evaluate others—when I, to recall Nietzsche's description of the masterful blond beast, set my own will up as the final arbiter of value. But it's precisely this will that's surrendered in self-emptying compassion for another. Recognition of the other's personhood prepares the way for the letting-go of judgmentalism, and the empathic union brought about by compassion completes the process. Judgment gives way to the concern to alleviate suffering. It's utterly unimportant whether the suffering arises from foolish or even sinful choices. So what if the robbed and wounded man rashly ignored warnings against traveling the dangerous Jericho-Jerusalem route on his own? So what if he himself was a brigand who'd been betrayed by his companions in crime? What matters why the homeless person is huddled over his grate? The point is that suffering is here and now, immediately present, and that it diminishes its victim's well-being. For the person of compassion, this is the only thing that really counts.

Action

In the New Testament, two different words—*eleemon* and *oiktirmon*—refer to the state of being merciful or having mercy. But the terms aren't synonymous. *Oiktirmon* refers to an internal feeling or attitude of empathic sorrow at another's suffering. But *eleemon* designates both internal empathy and external action. Mercy as *oiktirmon* can be passively subjective. *Eleemon*, on the other hand, is never merely a private feeling, but is also a course of behavior that flows from compassion for another's plight.

Significantly, it's *eleemon*, never *oiktirmon*, that's used by New Testament authors when they speak of the merciful nature of God. Moreover, when Jesus describes the Good Samaritan as a person of mercy, the word he uses is *eleos*, the root of *eleemon*. God's mercy is an active benevolence that enables rather than privately compassionates. It intervenes in the affairs of humans, deliberately reaching out to succor, heal, and midwife the new birth. Jesus' parable suggests that human *eleos* must likewise express itself in concrete behavior. Merely suffering-with in compassionate empathy isn't enough. Our compassion must work to enable individuals ravaged by suffering to come into their own as persons. When the sick, the lame, the blind, the oppressed, and the broken in spirit cry to Jesus, *"Kyrie eleison!"*— they're not simply asking for *oiktirmon*. They're pleading for actual help to overcome whatever holds them back from life, from being, from the new birth.

The Good Samaritan was well aware of the need to follow up compassion with action. The parable doesn't merely say he empathized with the roadside victim. It explicitly states that he

> went to him and bound up his wounds, pouring on oil and wine; then he set him on his own beast and brought him to an inn, and took care of him. And the next day he took out two denarii and gave them to the innkeeper, saying, "Take care of him; and whatever more you spend, I will repay you when I come back." (Luke 10:34–35)

If we read between the lines, three noteworthy points about merciful action emerge from this passage. The first is that the psychological sacrifice of self-interest by which compassion makes room for the sufferings of the other must be paralleled by a *material sacrifice* of time, energy, and resources. The Samaritan takes the time and exerts the energy to personally nurse the stricken man. He also willingly gives of his own possessions—the wine, the oil, and the denarii—to attend to the man's sufferings. Cheap mercy, of course, knows nothing of this. Distancing, not doing, is its characteristic mode of response. But the loving-kindness of genuine mercy can rest content with nothing less than an all-out effort to succor the neighbor. We're not just called upon to *forgive* seventy times seven, but to *give* seventy times seven as well, and this means a generously profligate expenditure of all that one has for the sake of the neighbor. And who is my neighbor? The parable of the Good Samaritan gives a clear answer: *everyone*. No person is an object, not the psychotic bag lady, not Roscoe, not the acquaintance who irritates me, nor even the criminal whose violent ill-will threatens me. *Eleos* makes them all equally my neighbors and thus proper recipients of my time, energy, and goods.

The second point about compassionate action is that it's *steadfastly committed* to the well-being of its recipient. The Samaritan instructed the innkeeper to tend to the roadside victim in his absence, and made it clear he would return to settle accounts and resume personal care of the man. Cheap mercy tends to consider its obligations met with one-shot expenditures: I toss a buck to the homeless person, I write a check to a charitable organization, I work one weekend at a food bank, and my sense of duty is satisfied. I've done my bit; what more could anyone expect of me?

But the compassionate action born of true *eleos* doesn't operate from this clock-punching mentality. It desires the genuine well-being of its recipient, and this means cultivating a long-term relationship with him or her to make sure that future needs aren't overlooked by focusing too closely on immediate ones. Mercy is a commitment, entered into with heart and soul, to lovingly stay the course, to stick it out for the long run. My neighbor continues to be my neighbor, and his or her personhood remains joined to mine by virtue of our shared connection to God. Consequently, as the Samaritan saw, my commitment to my neighbor's enablement should likewise endure, just as God's commitment to mine does.

Finally, compassionate action is its *own reward*. There's not even the slightest hint in Jesus' parable that the Samaritan expected some kind of return on his rescue of the stricken man from either the victim himself or God. The reason for this is simple: genuine *eleos* sees compassionate action as a joyous opportunity to midwife, not a grim responsibility. When forced to actually do something, howsoever minimal, cheap mercy grinds its teeth and resents the imposition. It's not surprising, then, that it expects some payoff for its pitying largesse, some concrete assurance that the effort has been worthwhile: either profuse gratitude on the part of the recipient or public acclaim. At the very least, it requires a guarantee that the investment isn't going to be squandered by the recipient—that the street person, for example, will use the buck tossed him to buy food instead of a bottle of cheap wine or a pack of smokes.

But the genuinely merciful person never feels imposed upon, because he or she knows herself indebted to the recipient of her compassionate action rather than the other way around. Peter

Maurin, who along with Dorothy Day founded the Catholic Workers, once remarked that we should be grateful for the needy, because their very destitution provides us with a blessed opportunity to pass on the enabling gift of loving-kindness given us by God.[20] The merciful person knows this. He or she doesn't think of her expenditure of self and goods as an investment, but as an occasion to nurture the same rebirth in others she herself has experienced. This doesn't mean she's pollyannaish about either the suffering or sacrifice compassionate action entails. But loving-kindness is willing to endure hardship for the sake of cooperating with God in the redemptive act of enablement.

The Circle of Mercy

The goal of Christianity is personhood in the fullest sense of the word. As we've seen, mercy is the midwife of personhood because it looks beyond outward appearances to discern the subject, made in God's likeness, embedded in each human being. Mercy celebrates the subject, and in its celebration seeks to enable the subject to recognize himself for what he is and arrive at the new birth that reestablishes his original relationship with God. "If anyone is in Christ, he is a new creation" (2 Cor 5:17).

Because each person is our neighbor—because each, even the Levite and the priest, shares our connectedness to God—Christian mercy seeks to extend ever wider the orbit of enabling loving-kindness. When it comes to mercy, there is no "us" and "them." As Jesus taught and Paul repeated, the fullness of personhood is the God-given right of all individuals, Jews and Gentiles, Christians and non-Christians, saints and sinners alike (Gal 3:27–28). No one is outside the circle.

In concrete terms, this means that mercy has to be practiced at both the individual and the social level. Our immediate response must and should be to those whom we meet on a one-to-one basis in our daily lives. But because everyone is our neighbor, whether or not we're personally acquainted with them, and because an integral component of compassionate action is concern for future as well as present well-being, the person of mercy can't stop with individual acts. He or she must stretch lovingkindness to work for the long-term good of all persons, those who now exist, as well as those who come afterwards. This necessarily calls the person of mercy to be a willing partner in social and perhaps even political efforts to reform oppressive institutions and policies.

The German theologian Helmut Thielicke makes this point in a provocative modern sequel to the Good-Samaritan parable. Thielicke imagines the Samaritan extending the circle of mercy far beyond the suffering man at the roadside. Aflame with the compassion born from genuine *eleos*, the Samaritan offers his love to the robbers as well. Why did they turn to crime in the first place? Surely, he reasons, because of material poverty and its ensuing despair. So he goes to the mayor of Jericho and persuades him to enact social policies that can do something to improve the lives of people in the area: affordable housing, job opportunities, better education, reliable health services, parks, libraries. Then the Samaritan selflessly devotes the rest of his days to making sure that everyone has the chance to profit from these reforms— to be better humans, and hence, a bit closer to a recognition of their own personhood. He works with governmental and social agencies for the sake of concretely suffering victims everywhere, and he does all this out of mercy.[21]

Or how about an example closer to home? The recent horror this country has suffered at the hands of terrorists (a horror, it's worth pointing out, that other countries have endured for some time now) has brought out the best in us when it comes to compassionately recognizing victims and selflessly working to alleviate their suffering. The mercy displayed by rescue workers, firefighters, cops, and ordinary citizens is both inspiring and, in the profoundest sense of the word, saving.

But of course the mercy taught by Jesus must go farther than this, extending to the terrorists themselves. For some who lost loved ones, either in domestic terrorist attacks or in subsequent combat on the other side of the world, and even for some who simply feel oppressed by the new climate of anxiety, such an extension is unthinkable. How can one empathize with, much less be compassionate for, thugs who strike unexpectedly and indiscriminately? Yet we are called by Christ to do so. We are called to *merciful recognition* by trying to put ourselves in their shoes long enough to understand and feel the pain and rage boiling within them. We're called to *merciful compassion* through our recognition of the brokenness of their own lives. And we're called to *merciful action* to work for economic and diplomatic reforms that alleviate the conditions which terrorists see as intolerably unjust. Succoring the victims of terrorism is but the first step in practicing mercy. Laboring for justice and peace, so that the conditions that encourage such brutal acts of rage are eliminated, finishes the job. As the parable of the Good Samaritan suggests, the true test is not how you treat those you like. The true test is how well you love those branded as enemies.

This kind of activism isn't merely one option among others for the Christian. If a Christian takes the fifth Beatitude seriously, it's a necessity. The Church has always taught that the faithful should be lights to the world in both word and deed, and nowhere is this more the case than when it comes to reproaching and resisting social structures that allow or even encourage some members of society to be degraded to the status of things. The activism fueled by *chesed* should always be undertaken in the name of love and compassion, intentionally eschewing a repetition of the anger and violence that give rise to oppressive social structures in the first place. Moreover, it should always keep its eye focused on persons rather than abstract principles. Otherwise, the risk of falling prey to the sentimentalist fallacy of the pity-giver looms large. But with these cautions ever in mind, genuine Christian mercy calls us forth to witness to the faith in the social arena as well as in personal relationships, gladly giving ourselves to enable the personhood of all our neighbors: those who endure suffering in the present, those who otherwise might endure suffering in the future; the young, the old, and those as yet unborn. The circle encompasses them all.

And it encompasses God as well, for all humans are members of God's body, and in enabling them to become fully persons, we likewise enable God to become fully God. When this happens, the circle of mercy is completed, and the saving grace of the Incarnation realized. But we must turn to our final chapter for a closer look at this mystery.

CHAPTER THREE

Merciful Meekness

...and the lion shall lie down with the lamb.
Isaiah 11:6

Lions and Lambs

I hope the preceding chapters have done something to show
that our Nietzschean culture's rejection of meekness and mercy as
morally repugnant is wrong-minded. Christian meekness is not a
rationalization for slavish timidity, nor is Christian mercy a
manipulative pity. Instead, both are gifts of grace necessary for
our spiritual growth. The one attunes us to the will of God. The
other, reflecting as it does God's creative midwifery of all creation, is an enabler of new birth.

Now it's time to consider Nietzsche's final criticism. This
charge, recall, is that even if meekness and mercy turn out not to
be morally repugnant, they're still so incompatible that any spirituality that takes them seriously is inherently self-contradictory.
Meekness is a lamb most comfortable in the green pastures of
quiet gentleness and withdrawn contemplation. Mercy is a roaring lion that robustly engages with the world. The Christian may

opt for one or the other, but any effort to incorporate both in one's spiritual life is bound to fail: meekness pushes us in one direction, mercy pulls us in another. The consequence is an internal civil war. Lions and lambs don't suffer one another's presence gladly.

Even those of us who conclude that Nietzsche missed the mark with his earlier criticisms of meekness and mercy may give reluctant assent to this one. In spite of our openly professed fidelity to meekness *and* mercy, the apparent incompatibility between them is deeply vexing. Many of us see no way of reconciling them, and so gradually tend to gravitate toward the one more in tune with our individual temperaments. Either the lamb sedates and declaws the lion, or the lion out-bellows the lamb. But this move is dangerous from both a private and public perspective. It skews our personal spiritual growth, forsaking *integritas* for lopsidedness, and it engenders theological and doctrinal rifts in the Body of Christ, dividing its members between competing interpretations of what the Christian way is "really" all about. This battle between the lamb and the lion has raged in the Church as well as within the hearts of individual Christians for two millennia.

The suspicion that meekness and mercy are fundamentally at odds with one another is, then, one which must be seriously examined. If we do so, however, we discover that it's without warrant. When understood correctly, meekness and mercy are perfectly compatible. Even stronger, they're so intimately interwoven that they actually depend upon one another. A Christian cannot be genuinely meek without also acting mercifully; merciful action can only arise on a foundation of meekness. Notwithstanding their differences, the lion of mercy and the lamb of meekness are intended to lie peaceably with one another. The two are so seamlessly related, in fact, that we properly ought not to refer to them separately. Instead, we should think of them as comprising a single spiritual virtue: "merciful meekness."

But what's the tie that binds them together? Our earlier discussions of the deep meaning of meekness and mercy have prepared us for the answer. The secret lies in a passage from one of Paul's letters: "Where the Spirit of the Lord is, there is freedom" (2 Cor 3:17). The nature of spiritual gifts such as meekness and mercy is that they *liberate* us to be the sons and daughters of God we are. Freedom is the middle term that connects meekness and mercy. Meekness is the gift of *freedom from* the obstacles that stand in the way of our coming into personhood. Mercy is the gift of *freedom to* grow in that personhood and to enable others to do likewise. Meekness strikes off our shackles, mercy teaches us how to walk without them. When we practice merciful meekness, we enter into the heart of what it means to be a Christian: a gratefully free and self-givingly creative co-worker in God's great plan of salvation.

But before we can fully appreciate the genuine liberty that merciful meekness brings, it's essential to get clear about what freedom *isn't*. And to do that, we must turn a final time to the Nietzschean perspective, for its characterization of freedom gives voice to what many of us implicitly endorse.

False Freedom

Our culture tends to view freedom as a phenomenon that begins and ends with the self. The rhetoric of freedom revolves around therapeutic expressions such as "self-control," "self-reliance," "self-sufficiency," "self-direction," and "self-determination," with the ultimate goal being "independence" or "autonomy." Sounds good, doesn't it? But a little reflection reveals that the undercurrent running beneath this rhetoric is the desire to exercise a Nietzschean will to power, to ramrod through anything perceived as a threat to either our wishes or behavior. When seen in this light, the autonomy at which the will to power aims is really a freedom *from* whatever gets in the way of self-assertion, and a freedom *to* unchecked license.

That this is the case should be clear from our earlier exploration of the ways in which we share to one degree or another Nietzsche's disdain of meekness and mercy. Although we profess allegiance to meekness, we secretly suspect it's a slavish timidity that holds us back from a masterfully uninhibited embrace of basic and "healthy" instincts. Meek persons surrender in the great battle of life by withdrawing from the struggle and retreating into the sanctuary of self-deceptive security. They lack the determination to overcome obstacles in a straightforward and manly fashion, just as they lack the courage to allow their deep-seated instinctual urges free reign. So they indenture themselves to the safe norms and values of the herd, and live out their pathetic lives in bondage.

In a similar way, our public professions of mercy are belied by our private suspicions that mercy—or "pity"—hopelessly entangles us in the petty miseries of those unfortunates who can't successfully compete for a place in the sun. If we take mercy on others, we not only don't do anything substantial to alleviate their sufferings—their condition, after all, is the result of a constitutional and hence incurable weakness—we also squander our own energies in the process, deflecting them from their proper focus: our own self-aggrandizement. The bestowal of mercy, then, interferes with our autonomy. If we allow ourselves to be on the receiving end of mercy, we likewise relinquish our freedom, because recipients of pity are debtors, forever unable to repay what they owe. Either way, mercy traps us in relationships that impede self-determination. In the brutal struggle for survival and success, one either runs with the pack dogs or soars like a solitary eagle.

What this suggests is that we tend to think of freedom as radical individualism. The free person—the master—refuses to answer to any authority but his or her own; distrusts personal involvement with others unless there's something in it for him; cultivates indifference to the weaknesses of others lest he or she be dragged down to their miserable level; single-mindedly charts his own course, relying on nothing but his personal physical and mental strength to get him through; and dares to plunge headfirst into life, regardless of the consequences to anyone else, in order to drink deeply and passionately of experience. The rugged individual, the Marlboro cowboy-type master, goes it alone, allowing his or her instinctual urges full sway, trusting that he and he alone has the stamina and insight to plot his own course. In Nietzschean terms, the free person is one who dares to exercise the will to power.

That this kind of rugged individualism is an ideal in our society can hardly be denied. We teach our kids to "think for themselves," to never let anyone "pull anything over on them," and to scramble for the golden ring of success with single-minded resolve. At the same time, in a perfectly consistent fashion, we warn them away from romantic relationships we fear may stifle their freedom, or from career decisions we think won't afford them maximum opportunity for self-determination. We ourselves bristle at the slightest perceived infringement of our own individualism, whether it comes from Washington or our boss or the pulpit. "Get your nose out of my business!"..."Keep your opinions to yourself!"..."Who do you think you are to tell me what to do?"..."A man's home is his castle"..."Good walls make good neighbors"..."Don't tread on me!"..."I'm the master of my fate and the captain of my soul": these and dozens of other snarling challenges or hackneyed platitudes attest to the fact that our culture is fixated on the assumption that freedom is equivalent to a noble individualism that demands to be left alone to pursue its own course. And this folk wisdom, at the end of the day, is nothing more than the rhetoric of Nietzsche's stalwartly untouchable master.

But the truth of the matter is that this understanding of freedom as radical individualism, alluring though it may be, is a false one. It fails as both a description of what we are and a prescription of how we should be.

In the first place, we simply aren't the rugged individualists we fancy ourselves. Twenty-five-hundred years ago, Aristotle famously said that a human is a *zoon politikon*, a political or social animal. As communal creatures, we don't take well to self-enclosed isolation. Like most primates, we need relationships with others to physically survive and psychologically flourish. Yet the Nietzschean notion of freedom insists that autonomy is attained only by ruthlessly cutting all significant interpersonal ties. Other humans are either slaves who threaten the master's freedom by trapping him in their petty concerns and chronic misery, or they're masters whose competing strength poses a threat to his sovereignty. In either case, the only proper way to maintain independence is by severing relations and striking out on one's own. Any association with either subordinates or peers only gets in the way of a full exercise of one's will to power and identity as an autonomous individual. But as Aristotle correctly observed, this attitude unnaturally goes against the grain of the kind of creatures we are. No person is a self-contained island.

The truth is that our need for relationship goes even deeper than Aristotle suspected. We're not just physically and psychologically connected with other humans. We're also bound by a much more significant and intimate tie: the spiritual bond of personhood. All of us share a common pedigree: the original unity with God. This oneness is indissoluble, despite our misguided efforts to shatter it, and it mysteriously links us with one another as well as the Source from which we came and in whose likeness we're made. As persons, we're extensions of the divine Person and of one another. God incarnated among us so that we could learn to recognize God in a human face, and in doing so we also come to recognize our own faces. In mercifully succoring broken wayfarers, we not only minister to God, we also minister to ourselves. It cannot be otherwise in a personal universe. As St. Paul realized, communion, not isolation, is the order of things: "For as in one body we have many members, and all the members do not have the same function, we, though many, are one body in Christ, and individually members one of another" (Rom 12:4–5). However else genuine freedom can be described, then, it most emphatically is not the detached self-sufficiency of the Nietzschean individualist.

Moreover, the freedom of rugged individualism is as misguided a prescription of how humans *ought* to be as it is a false description of how we in fact *are*. The reason for this should now be obvious: Because the self-imposed isolation of the will-to-powered master is unnatural, it's also ultimately destructive. The attempt to sever all ties with God and fellow humans doesn't give rise to the fulfillment that Nietzsche and like-minded individualists exultantly promise. On the contrary, it stunts our development into persons—that is, into creatures who have rediscovered true being in the new birth—by exiling us to a forlorn tundra of lonely and directionless egoism. Thrown back upon him- or herself, utterly disconnected from the original unity that allows communion both horizontally with others and vertically with God, the individualist might achieve a certain degree of freedom *from* messy relationships that distract her self-absorption, as well as some freedom *to* allow her instincts to run wild. But the price required for this false freedom is so high that no reasonable person would either pay it or advise anyone else to do so.

White Pebbles

Our earlier explorations of Nietzsche's repudiation of meekness and mercy have already cited many passages that illustrate his understanding of freedom as will-to-powered individualism. In this chapter, let's turn instead to a novel that both accurately expresses the essence of his position and dramatically underscores its exorbitant cost to the human spirit. The novel is André Gide's *The Immoralist*. The book, published in 1921, never mentions Nietzsche by name. But it's clearly an attempt to push Nietzsche's masterly freedom to its logical conclusion by imaginatively recounting the life of Michel, a young man who transforms himself through sheer will power into a blond beast. That this is Gide's intention is underscored by the novel's title. Nietzsche was fond of ironically referring to both himself and his master types as "immoralists": persons who have dared to liberate themselves from the stultifying values of the Christian herd.

When we first meet Michel, he's exactly the kind of person Nietzsche would scornfully dismiss as a slave: physically weak, emotionally repressed, timidly withdrawn from the world. Raised by a bookish father, Michel was something of a child prodigy. While still in his teens, he mastered half a dozen ancient languages and established a reputation as a brilliant historian. Gide's symbolism is obvious here: Michel is more comfortable with dead languages and vanished civilizations than he is with the vibrantly throbbing world of passionate instinct. He prefers the safety of detached observation to the riskier business of living. As Michel himself confesses, "I reached the age of twenty-five, having barely cast a glance at anything but books and ruins and knowing nothing of life."[1]

But then two events change everything. The first is marriage. Shortly before his death, Michel's father arranges for his son to wed a young woman named Marceline. Michel has no real desire for the union, but assents to it in order to please his father. The second event is Michel's own near-death. On his honeymoon trip (the bookworm Michel unromantically drags his bride to northern Africa so that he can examine some ancient ruins) he falls so ill with galloping consumption that the local doctors give him up for lost. At first Michel passively accepts their prognosis and prepares himself for death. This, of course, is entirely in keeping with his character. He's never been good at self-assertion or resistance. His usual response has been to buckle "meekly" before anything fate throws at him. But after hovering between darkness and light for a few weeks, Michel discovers deep within himself a hitherto-unexperienced lust for life, an overwhelming desire to make a fresh start, to replace his old bookish timidity with lion-hearted strength and passion. "Death had touched me," he says, and "I came to think it a very astonishing thing to be alive....Before, thought I, I did not understand I was alive. The thrilling discovery of life was...mine."[2]

Michel resolves that his struggle to survive and transform himself into a new man must be totally unaided. It's a battle he and he alone must fight. True, he accepts some physical nursing from Marceline so long as she doesn't "interfere" with his "renascent life." But the real life-restoring tonic is his own determination. "It is a matter of will," he asserts. "I strengthened my will as one strengthens one's memory by revising a lesson; I instructed my hostility, directed it against all and sundry; I was to fight with everything; my salvation depended on myself alone."[3] When Michel insists his rebirth is entirely up to him, he means it. At one point during his convalescence, he discovers that his wife has been praying for his recovery, and he explodes in protest:

"You mustn't pray for me, Marceline. I don't want favors."

"Do you reject the help of God?"

"He would have a right to my gratitude afterwards. It entails obligations. I don't like them."[4]

Fantastically, against all odds, Michel's struggle for self-birth succeeds. His old bookish, life-denying identity dies along with the last tuberculosis bacillus, and a new Michel emerges, one who feels the will to power surging through his vitals and eager to let loose all the tumultuous passions and instincts the old Michel fearfully repressed. To signal his reawakened "impulse toward a wilder, more natural state,"[5] Michel shaves his scholar's beard, tans his body under the hot Algerian sun, and allows his hair— the mane of a roaring lion—to grow long.

One of the insights granted him by his "wilder, more natural state" is that the only mode of freedom worthy of a self-born master is ruthless detachment from others. Self-reliance is the key to liberty, Michel decides, and it's won only by going it alone. So, just as he earlier forbade Marceline to pray because he refused to be obliged to God, he now severs potentially indebting contact with old companions and friends. There's an additional reason as well: Typical of a master, Michel has decided that the herd (and all his acquaintances, he now concludes, are herdsmen) is subhuman, and he wants above all to avoid being contaminated by it. The common run of people, terrified of anything that smacks of real passion or instinctual vitality, "seem to be alive, and yet not to know they are alive." Their entire ethos of self-denying meekness and mercy is a "destroyer of life" and an inhibitor of freedom.

> [M]ost of them believe that it is only by constraint they can get any good out of themselves, and so they live in a state of psychological distortion. It is his own self that each of them is most afraid of resembling. Each of them sets up a pattern and imitates it; he doesn't even choose the pattern he imitates; he accepts a pattern that has been chosen for him.... The fear of finding oneself alone—that is what they suffer from—and so they don't find themselves at all. I detest such moral agoraphobia—the most odious cowardice, I call it.[6]

Bit by bit, with relentless thoroughness, Michel resists moral agoraphobia by cutting his ties with everyone—the contemptible herd, detestable "people of principle,"[7] and scholarly bookworms who merely read and write about life, as he once did, but never exuberantly throw themselves into it. He even begins to distance himself from Marceline. He uncomfortably realizes that her faithful care of him during his illness places him in her debt, and debt is one thing a blond beast can't abide. It encroaches upon the conceit of absolute self-sufficiency. Now the only companions Michel will suffer are ruffians who live by their instinct and cunning rather than by the enfeebling herd rules. And as he removes himself more and more from those who would pull him down to their level, he believes himself progressively attuned to previously "untouched treasures" in his own will to power, treasures that had almost been "covered up, hidden, smothered by culture and decency and morality."[8]

But along with his newly discovered treasures comes an increasing restlessness, an escalating need to divorce himself totally from the smothering company of the "culture and decency and morality" that threatens his majestic autonomy. He begins to wander throughout Europe, reluctantly tolerating the company of his wife, in search of the wide open space he craves. When he fails to find it—Europe, after all, is rotten with culture and decency and morality—he returns to northern Africa, where his self-birth took place, moving from one remote village to the next.

The frenetic pace of traveling weakens Marceline, and she soon shows signs of the consumption that had almost carried off Michel. He tries to nurse her as she once tended him, but he can't hide his revulsion at her sickly dependence. Shortly before her death, Marceline says to him, "I quite understand your doctrine…; but it does away with the weak." Unable to contain himself, Michel blurts out: "And so it should!"[9] When Marceline dies, she dies alone. The blond beast Michel, utterly revolted by the sickroom that reeks of decay and weakness, has crept away to prowl about in the desert night. With the burial of his wife, Michel finally shakes off the final impediment to his absolute freedom. His rebirth is complete. At last he's achieved what he wanted.

Or at least what he *thought* he wanted. For at the novel's end, the Michel we encounter is anything but a joyfully roaring blond beast. Instead, he's an empty shell, adrift in the world, confused and rudderless. He's won radical autonomy. He's become the completely independent individualist, needing no one, owing no one, giving to no one. But the freedom to which he's broken through is as empty and featureless as the African desert he secludes himself in. "I have reached a point in my life beyond which I cannot go," he tells us. "I can no longer understand things....To know how to free oneself is nothing; the arduous thing is to know what to do with one's freedom."[10] Writing to a couple of old acquaintances to whom he turns in desperation, Michel plaintively begs them: "Take me away from here and give me some reason for living. I have none left. I have freed myself. That may be. But what does it signify? This objectless liberty is a burden to me."[11] The final chilling impression we're left with is of an exhausted man for whom purpose has withered and meaning crumbled, whose existence is utterly futile:

> Look! I have here a number of white pebbles. I let them soak in the shade, then hold them in the hollow of my hand and wait until their soothing coolness is exhausted. Then I begin once more, changing the pebbles and putting back those that have lost their coolness to soak in

the shade again....Time passes and the evening comes
on...[12]

With Michel, the Nietzschean chickens have come home to
roost. Freedom as untrammeled individualism, freedom as absolute
liberation from the ties of human relationships, freedom as
unchecked indulgence of the "wilder, more natural" instincts—this
kind of freedom creates a spiritual vacuum. The "self-sufficient"
master loses his way in the empty desert of his own ego. Having
isolated himself from any meaningful relationship with others or
God, he likewise loses touch with who he really is. His liberty
becomes a burden, as Michel realized too late, because it is void
of authentic connection or commitment. Will to power eventually
turns against its wielder. "You have me!" it mocks. "But only at the
price of everything, including your own soul. Now what?" At the
end of the day, the ruggedly individualistic blond beast has no
answer to this question. Like Michel, he can only sit in exhausted
bewilderment, absently clutching and releasing lifeless pebbles.

Freedom's Double Movement

Michel's sad fate unforgettably shows up the spurious nature
of Nietzschean freedom. Plowing one's way through life with the
battering ram of will to power is foolishly destructive. Clutching
at a majestically self-contained and isolated autonomy inevitably
leads to dry-mouthed hollowness. How could it not? In shutting
ourselves off from others and God, we violate our original oneness
and necessarily plunge from being toward nothingness. Thus the
liberating self-birth the master strives for is an illusory dead-end.
As Merton reminds us, "to withdraw from where I am in order to
be totally outside all that situates me—this is real delusion."[13]

In contrast to our ethos's Nietzschean endorsement of radically detached individualism, the Christian spiritual tradition maintains that genuine liberation is possible only through committed interaction with God and our fellow human beings. Concretely situated engagements, both horizontally and vertically, are the horizons of our freedom. Liberation is found within these parameters or not at all. Christian freedom is not a matter of punching one's way through any and all relationships to become an untouchably autonomous individualist, but rather of operating within them to discover and embrace one's true identity.

When we do so, we immediately discover that Christian freedom is not at all the one-dimensional independence championed by Nietzscheans. On the contrary, it's so complex as to appear paradoxical. In writing of it, Paul tells us that "he who was called in the Lord as a slave is a freedman of the Lord. Likewise, he who was free when called is a slave of Christ" (1 Cor 7:22). Peter says something quite similar. "Live as free men," he encourages us. "But live as servants of God" as well (1 Pet 2:16). The implication of both these texts is that Christian liberation somehow frees on the one hand, but enslaves on the other. Martin Luther hammered home the apparent paradoxicality of Paul's and Peter's words by crystallizing them in this well-known formula: "A Christian is a perfectly free lord of all, subject to none. A Christian is a perfectly dutiful servant of all, subject to all."[14]

But the paradox dissolves once we realize that the situationally engaged freedom proclaimed by Christianity contains a double movement. Peter, Paul, and Luther are not claiming that the Christian is *simultaneously* subservient slave and free lord, but rather that the two states are *consecutively* related to one another. Genuine Christian freedom is only attainable if we first subordinate ourselves to God, acknowledging his superiority and following his lead. When we willingly bow the knee and confess ourselves "servants of God," we achieve freedom *from* the ensnarements of self-will and arrogant egoism that so cripple the would-be master. In relinquishing the false freedom of self-sufficiency, we experience the true liberation of servanthood. This is the first movement of Christian freedom. The second is this: Once our own will is suborned to divine will, we become empowered to act in the world in a godly fashion. Drawn by our servanthood into the fuller being of personhood, we attain freedom *to* enable others in their own rebirth.

It's worth pointing out that the Nietzschean dimly grasps the double movement of genuine freedom. But blinded as he is by illusions of self-mastery, he fails to appreciate what it entails. He presumes that freedom from bondage means aloof separation rather than a situated commitment to serve God, and just as misguidedly takes the freedom to enable the flourishing of other concretely situated humans as a mandate to focus exclusively on his own interests and instinct-gratification. Similarly, the Nietzschean has a glimmering that freedom brings new birth. Yet like Michel, he arrogantly assumes that the rebirth is self-generated, rather than a spiritual gift bestowed by divine grace.

We're now in a position to see just how inseparably connected meekness and mercy really are, and how both of them are invitations to reestablish the original oneness necessary for integrated personhood. Christian meekness is precisely the alignment of our will with God's that constitutes the first movement of genuine freedom. When we confess our inability to quell the beast of self-will; when we know ourselves so impoverished that we're utterly reliant on the grace of God to pull us through; when

we acknowledge our dependence with gratitude and humility—
when we admit all this, we enter into the way of meekness and
are thereby liberated from the beast's ravages.

Then, when God mercifully rescues us from our destitution
by lovingly enabling us to reverse our backward slide into nothingness to a forward thrust aimed at the full being of personhood,
we enter the second movement of Christian freedom. Our con-
fessed dependency on God empowers us to recognize ourselves
as the God-imaged persons we truly are. This in turn frees us to
recognize that others share our Godlikeness, and inspires us to
nurture their growth into *integritas* by creatively midwifing them
in the same way God midwifed us. God reaches down to our concrete condition of self-willed bondage to liberate us with the servanthood of meekness, mercifully loving us into being so that we
in turn might reach out to the concretely situated suffering of
others with his free gift of mercy.

To put all this in the language of scripture, we need only turn
to the writings of St. Paul, especially his autobiographical Letter
to the Romans. This epistle is not only a record of Paul's own
search for spiritual freedom. It's also the central Christian reflection on what it means to be liberated by merciful meekness.

For Paul, as for Karl Rahner, the goal of a Christian is to
rediscover his or her original oneness with God and thus partake,
as God intended, of the fullness of being. That this is even necessary in the first place is due to the fact that humans have ruptured the primal relationship through disobedient self-will.
Although I've not used the word to this point, Paul unhesitantly
calls such willful rebellion *sin*. We fall into sin when we fancy ourselves (to invoke Nietzschean terms) masterful lords in total control of our own destiny. We allow the beast free reign under the

false presumption that freedom consists of doing whatever we wish whenever we wish, and that so long as we muster the requisite will to power, we're invulnerable.

But sin is deceitful (Heb 3:13). It beguiles us with promises of self-determination and strength, yet delivers just the opposite. The more leeway we give the passions—Nietzsche's "healthy instincts"—the more enslaved we become to their incessant demands for gratification (Rom 6:12). Such enslavement is as insidious as a chemical addiction. We tell ourselves that we're in charge, that we're in command of things, but in fact it's we who are commanded. We hop on the tiger's back with arrogant confidence that he can be steered. But the tiger quickly begins to go his own way—this is what tigers do—and before long we're incapable either of directing him or dismounting.

The upshot is that the tiger takes us ever deeper into the tangled jungle of sinful bondage and away from the pellucid clearing of oneness with God. The longer we ride the tiger's back, the more we move from full being toward the horrible nothingness that defines separation from God. Everything that exists does so only because it borrows its being from the divine Source of being, and humans are no exception. The closer our relationship to the Source, the more complete our being; the more fragmented the relationship, the lesser our being. Thus rebellious self-will—sin— not only enslaves the sinner, but progressively hurtles him or her away from God toward nonbeing, or nothingness. And what else is this rupture of oneness and subsequent slide into forlorn nothingness, asks Paul, but spiritual death? The wages of sin are death (Rom 6:23); the sting of death is sin (1 Cor 15:56).

Still, as Nietzsche properly reminds us, humans have a seemingly inexhaustible capacity for self-deception or rationalization.

So we frequently try to delude ourselves into thinking that our relationship with God is healthy if we outwardly conform to the dictates of religious or ethical law. This, of course, is precisely the route Paul himself took before his conversion. But so long as we're on the tiger's back of self-will, conformity to the Law is nothing more than just another expression of sinful and hence deadly rebellion.

It's not that the Law itself is sinful, but that we misuse it as an opportunity for sin (Rom 7:8–11). This is because our conformity to it doesn't spring from a selfless desire to please God, but rather from the will-to-powered urge to secure our own position. We go through the motions of obedience, but do so only to feed our own insatiable egoism: in this case, the arrogant conceit that we're better than anyone else because we, unlike they, are self-disciplined and strong enough to run the obstacle course of the Law. We use the Law for our own ends and, as a consequence, our "fidelity" to it only feeds the beast of self-will. Thus the very "sinful passions...at work in our members to bear fruit for death," which we fancy we've controlled, in fact are further "aroused" by our abuse of the Law (Rom 7:5). The enslaving shackles of sin tighten their grip, the slide into spiritual death accelerates.

If the wages of self-willed disobedience (whether the disobedience is unabashedly open or disguised as fidelity to the Law) are slavery and death, the way out is through surrender and obedience. This, and this only, can reestablish the original oneness with God ruptured by our waywardness. But as we saw in chapter 1, we can't bootstrap our way into surrender and obedience. Willful attempts to tame the beast only strengthen it. So God mercifully gives us a helping hand with the spiritual gift of *meekness*: the radical openness to divine will that comes from the desolate awareness of our self-destructive tendencies and our utter dependence on grace. Just as God graciously gave us the gift of his own death, so he graciously gives us the death of our self-will in the destitution of *ptoches*. The tiger is routed, our individual slates are wiped clean—just as humanity's slate was cleared by the death of Jesus—so that we might make a fresh start: "We know that our old self was crucified with him so that the sinful body might be destroyed, and we might no longer be enslaved to sin. For he who has died is freed from sin" (Rom 6:6–7).

Now, at first glance the obedient surrender of our will to God's that constitutes meekness might seem nothing more than a transition from one form of bondage to another. And, indeed, Paul even says as much: "Having been set free from sin, [you] have become slaves of righteousness" (Rom 6:18). Yet we must remember that meekness is but the first movement of Christian liberation. For in dying as Christ died and becoming a servant of God, we additionally, through the grace of divine mercy, are rejuvenated as Christ was: "As Christ was raised from the dead by the glory of the Father, we too...walk in newness of life" (Rom 6:4).

This "newness of life" is the rebirth into which God midwives us, the reestablishment of our original oneness with the Source of our being. Our freedom *from* the dominion of sin through meekness, then, liberates us and gives us the freedom *to* be "alive to God in Christ Jesus" (Rom 6:11). But to be reborn in this way means that Christ lives in us, and we are suffused with the same kind (although not the same degree) of life-giving mercy that midwifed us back into being. We are freed to emulate the loving-kindness of *eleos*—freed to recognize the dormant Christ-self in others, freed to reach out to them in compassion rather than from the legalistic subterfuge of pity, freed to function as midwifing enablers of their own return to full being, freed to serve them in the way God in Christ serves us, without any expectation of return, even to the point of utter sacrifice. "I could wish that I myself were accursed and cut off from Christ for the sake of my brethren" (Rom 9:3). We are, in a word, freed to be persons who reflect the merciful meekness of the divine Person.

Thus our meek servitude to God makes us a lord, and our lordship makes us a merciful servant to others. In the process, we achieve the *integritas* that is our destiny as children of God, an *integritas* that brings purpose and fulfillment undreamt of by pebble-clutching Michel and his fellow blond beasts. This is what true Christian freedom is all about. As St. Paul said, where the Spirit of the Lord is, there is freedom.

Contrary to our Nietzschean suspicions, then, meekness and mercy are not mutually exclusive. The lamb and the lion are not enemies, but partners who together offer us the gifts of personhood: freedom and being. Blessed are the mercifully meek, for to them is given the promise of oneness with God and neighbor.

Let's explore more fully the double movement toward free personhood that merciful meekness brings.

Wounded Openness

One of my basic claims in this book—a claim borrowed from Karl Rahner—has been that the ultimate goal of Christian spirituality is to nurture us into the full being of personhood. Personhood is a recovery of our original oneness with God, and this recovery is possible only when the spiritual gift of merciful meekness has liberated us *from* the beast of self-will and freed us *to* midwife others in loving-kindness.

An essential aspect of the freedom offered by merciful meekness, and hence, an essential aspect of personhood as well, is what Rahner calls an "unconditional acceptance of human existence" that allows us to embrace ourselves as the particular individuals we are. "Unconditional acceptance" means that we embrace without reservation both our strengths and weaknesses, beauty and blemishes, wholeness and brokenness, neither romantically whitewashing the bad nor cynically discounting the good. We are not spotlessly pure angels soaring in the ether or mere animals dumbly embedded in the physical order. We are humans, born with unique temperaments and complex personalities into concrete situations, but also made in the image of God. We are hybrids, if you will, possessing angelic tendencies that pull us upward as well as animalistic ones that draw us downward, and to unconditionally accept who and what we are means to be radically "open," as Rahner says, to both of them.[15]

It hardly needs pointing out that this is easier said than done. Honest self-appraisal doesn't come easily to most of us. Nietzsche is correct on that score at least. We tend to defensively overlook our own fragility and blow ourselves up into superhumans endowed with exclusively good qualities. Yes, yes, we impatiently admit if pushed to the wall; we do perhaps have one or two small weaknesses. But we're working on them. Besides, when compared to all our strengths, they're quite insignificant. We're okay—really we are!

But of course none of us is "really okay," are we? Every one of us carries deep emotional and psychological wounds that have been inflicted by our particular situations. Some of us are the victims of unhappy or even miserable childhoods; others reel from broken adult relationships. Some of us are crushed by the despair brought on by racism or poverty; others, ironically, are burdened by positions of social privilege or wealth. Regardless of the circumstances, no one is immune from fears, anxieties, and insecurities. We all have our dark and dirty secrets, our hidden blemishes. We may try to deny these wounds, but they still fester deeply within us, assaulting us outright with conscious pain or, more insidiously, with a below-the-surface sense of quiet desperation.

One of the merits of Nietzsche's attack on Christianity is his psychological insight that instead of getting in touch with these wounds, we usually try to repress them and thus anesthetize the suffering they bring. What he failed to appreciate, however, is that the very will to power he recommended as a way out is the most common strategy of wound-denial we invoke. We convince ourselves that the nagging hurts and throbbing gashes we carry can be healed on our own if we but exercise enough disciplined resolve. But willful attempts to bootstrap out of our wounds only feed the beast of self-will, and we become progressively enslaved to its destructive whims. The consequence is that we close down to both ourselves and others. Our desperate attempts to deny our own fragility blindside us to who we really are as concrete individuals, and our self-absorbed efforts to be invulnerable make us indifferent to the wounds of others. Our inability to honestly confess our own fragility kills the prospect of empathizing with anyone else's.

The gift of merciful meekness, as St. Paul discovered on the road to Damascus, liberates us from this horrible cycle of bondage by forcing us to acknowledge our woundedness. When we recognize the awful destitution of our *ptoches*, and meekly admit our need for outside help, we're freed to open up to a truth that until then would have struck us as sheer madness: that the very fragility we once deplored and struggled to deny is a great blessing, because in and through it we encounter the saving mercy of God. We comprehend, as Jean Vanier says, that we're "called to discover that God can bring peace, compassion, and love through our wounds," not in spite of them, that our wounds are actually conduits rather than obstacles to oneness and personhood.[16] And when this realization breaks in upon us, we're able to unconditionally accept—to freely embrace—our wounds as the opportunity for life they in fact are.

Nor does the gift stop there. Along with the meek acceptance of our own vulnerability comes a newly awakened recognition and merciful compassion for the wounds of others as well. Freed from the self-absorbed scramble to deny our own fragility, we are more receptive to the suffering that surrounds us. Moreover, our receptivity isn't the abstractly intellectual nod of the head characteristic of pity's cheap mercy, much less the self-serving conformity to abstract Law deplored by Paul, but rather a heartfelt empathy born from our confession of destitute dependency. When honestly acknowledged, our own suffering is a great eye-opener—or, better, heart-opener—that allows us to recognize the wounds of others. We unconditionally accept the fragility of others, not judging or condoning, but desiring only to lovingly share their wounds as extensions of our own.

The mercy we wish to give others can, of course, take many forms. Once again, humans are concretely situated, and mercy must work within those situations if it's to be effective. But regardless of the particular circumstances, mercy rides upon meekness to humbly expose our own wounds, our own brokenness and fears and anxieties and shame, to others. When we do this, we say to them: "I'm no better than you. I have no magic bullet to make your pain go away. I'm not an invincible or all-know-ing guru. But I'm willing, if you'll allow me, to open myself to your suffering. And I'm also willing to trust you enough to share mine with you, because we both need one another."

In a wonderfully insightful reading of the gospel story of Jesus and the woman at the well (John 4:7–18), Jean Vanier presses home the point that one of the mercy-giver's greatest gifts is his meek confession of vulnerability:

When Jesus meets her, he does not tell her to get her act together. Rather, he exposes to her his own need. He says to her: "Give me to drink." It is good to see how Jesus approaches broken people: not from a superior position but from a humbler, lower, position, even from his fatigue: "I need you."[17]

Vanier's gloss not only illustrates merciful meekness's uncon-ditional acceptance of humans as they are—Jesus accepts his own vulnerability just as he does the woman's—but reminds us too that the freedom merciful meekness brings is a rediscovery of our original oneness with God. Merciful meekness is a spiri-tual gift, and like all such gifts reflects the nature of its divine bestower.

As we've seen time and again in earlier chapters, we're called to practice meekness and mercy not simply because they're pleas-ing to God, but because they're godly attributes. The Sermon on the Mount, remember, is autobiographical theology. Jesus recom-mends meekness and mercy because they're his own qualities, and he desires us to be one with the Father as he is. In the spirit of unconditional acceptance's total openness, God in Christ met us where we were. He meekly took on human frailty and mercifully exposed that frailty to suffering humankind so that we might reawaken to our Godlike potential for freedom and personhood. By emptying himself of full Being, he brought to humans the gift of being, and along with that gift, the possibility of rebirth. He became one of us so that we might once again become one with him. As St. Paul says, God in Christ freed us through his merciful meekness for freedom (Gal 5:1): freedom *from* self-will and deception, freedom *to* become persons. In unconditionally accepting the gift of that freedom, we so attune ourselves to God that we continue the saving work of the Incarnation.

The wounded openness of Christian freedom, then, attests to the essential compatibility of meekness and mercy. God meekly withdraws from the full plenitude of his Being in order to mercifully share our frailty. When we experience the double movement of this gift, we meekly withdraw from the arrogantly clamorous demands of self-will so that we might open our hearts in empathic mercy to the frailty of others. First inward meekness, then outward mercy: God's freely given mode of relating is recapitulated at the human level. The lion and the lamb lie beside one another.

Powerful Weakness

Making contact through merciful meekness with our wounds allows us the freedom of openness. But it also helps us touch base with a second essential characteristic of genuinely free personhood: what Rahner describes as "the basic capacity of love," a capacity, moreover, that's "without measure." If our wounds speak to the fallen side of our nature, measureless love reminds us of the angelic side. When a person is freed to love, says Rahner, he's finally "caught up with himself and thus knows what is in him and who he is." He recognizes a greatness or "boundlessness" within himself that hitherto was "veiled" by his own waywardness, and fully "enters into the adventure of his own reality." This love both reflects and participates in God's creative loving-kindness, which mercifully brought him into being and continues to sustain him, and consequently, is a source of inexhaustible power. But it's a power that can only be realized by first openly acknowledging woundedness. Confession of weakness is a necessary condition for the boundless empowerment of love. The double movement once more reveals itself: first meekness, then mercy.[18]

We commonly speak of love as the "most powerful force in the world." So it is. But the nature of this power isn't as we ordinarily imagine it. What we generally have in mind is drawn from the literature of romantic ardor: a surge of passion so overwhelming that it impetuously tidal waves over any and all obstacles until the beloved for whom the heart burns is possessed. All of us have experienced this kind of ravenously churning passion; it's the stuff of poetry and song and film. Romantic troubadours sing its praises today just as they did in past generations. Young people yearn for its fire, elderly people nostalgically recall its scorching flame.

It's important to keep in mind, however, that the consuming blast of romantic love isn't the kind of power Rahner means when he writes about love as a boundless or measureless capacity of personhood. All too often (although certainly not always), love as romantic passion is a spasm of the old Nietzschean will to power, an eruption of the deep-seated desire to indulge in instinctual license. It is as explosive and unpredictably spontaneous as *phumos* (recall our discussion in chapter 1), leading us toward excesses that may provide some degree of immediate gratification but ultimately damage both ourselves and others. The unbridled self-assertion and urge to possess that are characteristic of such passion are, without doubt, extremely powerful. But it's not at all the power of Christian love. Romantic ardor is a frenzy that bulldozes its way to victory, and victory is typically defined in terms of seizure and possession of the beloved. Christian love, on the other hand, displays none of this will-to-powered machismo. As St. Paul said, it "does not insist on its own way." Instead, it is "patient and kind," "not jealous or boastful," "not arrogant or rude," "not irritable or resentful" (1 Cor 13:4–5).

The power of Christian love, a power "made perfect" in meekness (cf. 2 Cor 12:9–10), consists not in self-interested passionate explosions but rather in the merciful desire to sacrifice self-interest for the sake of the beloved. Its power lies in its capacity to midwife broken people back into the fullness of being, to enable them to acknowledge their own woundedness and in doing so to recognize their own boundlessness. Christian love continues the liberating gift of God's own self-emptying in the service of humanity. This gift, discovered in meekness and brought to fruition through mercy, is unimaginably powerful in the sense that it is measurelessly creative. And the fruit of its creativity is new life—or, as Paul tells us in his Letter to the Romans, freedom from the killing bondage of separation from God.

The creative power to mercifully enable new life characteristic of Christian love—an empowerment, keep in mind, made possible only through meekness—can be illustrated by taking another look at two persons already discussed in this book. The first is Henri Nouwen's Adam; the second is our old friend, the Good Samaritan.

Adam, you recall, was a youth so mentally and physically handicapped that, in the eyes of the world, he was totally powerless—an unfortunate, as Isaiah might have said, truly "despised and rejected." Unable to attend to even his simplest needs, he was utterly reliant on others not just for his daily maintenance but, literally, for his survival as well. In every sense of the word, Adam was a person of *ptoches*, of radical and relentless destitution.

To all outward appearances, then, Adam was hopelessly enslaved in the prison of his own disabilities. And, indeed, this was Nouwen's initial response when first assigned the task of caring for him. But as we saw, Nouwen gradually awakened to the fact that Adam was actually a living parable, a flesh-and-blood teaching of the blessedness of meekness. Adam's limitations freed him from the rapacious beast of self-will that assails stronger, more "able" types. He had no conceit of invulnerability, no anxious fears of being disdainfully condemned as an ineffectual mouse, no burning obsession to prove himself a blond beast. In Adam, there was no pretense, no public dissimulation, no challenge to others. His very mode of existence was a humble acknowledgment of his deep woundedness. He accepted his impoverishment, just as he accepted the necessity of aligning his will with that of his caretakers, because he realized in a dim way that his poverty was something over which he had no control, and that his subordination of will was ultimately for his own good. Adam unashamedly accepted his condition, and in that humility Nouwen discerned the presence of the lowly and despised Christ.

But Nouwen also discovered that Adam's unself-conscious meekness was a living exemplification of Jesus' promise that "he who is least among you is the one who is great" (Luke 9:48), for

Adam's very "brokenness" was a "witness to God's love."[19] His disabilities liberated him from the tiger of self-will the rest of us cling to, enabling him to love the people around him in an uncomplicatedly open way. There was no hidden agenda to Adam's love. It was given unstintingly, unreservedly, with all the innocent trust and confidence and goodwill of a child's love for her parents.

And when Nouwen grasped the purity of Adam's love, he himself drew strength from it. The young man's embrace of Nouwen just as he was—not the world-famous author and lecturer, but a man wrestling with his own wounded need for love—empowered Nouwen to come to terms with his own fragility and thereby touch base with "the ground of being" and "the source of life."[20] This, Nouwen discovered, was Adam's Christlike ministry: to mercifully midwife others, in and through his meekness, toward an awakening to their own personhood. In doing so, Adam became a vehicle of the divine loving-kindness that enables rebirth. His weakness was the opportunity for the liberating power of God's *eleos*. Although he couldn't know it, Adam's life of merciful meekness was a great *makarios* for Nouwen—and, through Nouwen, for us as well.

The power of love that comes only from genuine meekness is also the frequently overlooked message in the parable of the Good Samaritan. The Samaritan, like Adam—like Christ himself—was a person "despised and rejected." Yet from his wounds flowed the enabling power of merciful love.

Samaritans were scornfully dismissed as pariahs in Jesus' day. They were people of mixed blood, and hence, viewed as impure by Jews obsessed with legalistic purity. To touch a Samaritan or even come into contact with one was considered an act of uncleanliness that called for immediate ritualistic absolution. Jews traveling southward from the Galilee to Jerusalem regularly lengthened their journey to detour around Samaria. Merely walking on the region's soil was too much for them. It's little wonder that the woman at the well, herself a Samaritan, was startled by Jesus' request for a drink. What self-respecting Jew would accept water from unclean hands? "How is it that you, a Jew, ask a drink of me, a woman of Samaria?" (John 4:9).

The priest and the Levite who passed by the wounded man on the Jericho-Jerusalem road were properly observant Jews. We can never know, of course, precisely why they chose to ignore him. But if called to task for their refusal of mercy, they might have defended themselves by appealing to legalistic norms of cleanliness: contact with spilt blood was also an act of impurity that required absolution. The irony is that they would have invoked a similar standard to avoid personal contact with the perfectly unbloodied Samaritan had they met *him* on the road. They were pure, upright, covenanted men; he, a polluted outcast. To their self-righteous way of thinking, the Samaritan would have been no different than the unseemly mess groaning in the dust.

The Samaritan, just like his countrywoman who gave Jesus drink at the well, had no delusions about his status. He knew he was trash in the eyes of Jews, and the wounds inflicted by this knowledge were deep and hurtful. When he spied the wounded man, who presumably was a Jew, he could well have allowed those wounds to harden his heart. "To hell with you, pal! If I'm not good enough to sup with you, worship with you, or even walk on the same road as you, I'm certainly not good enough to nurse you! So just stay where you are until the buzzards pick your bones. You'll die, but at least you'll die a 'pure' man!"

But this isn't what happened. The Samaritan's pained awareness of his own vulnerability and weakness freed him to open up
to the wayfarer's plight. His own precarious destitution liberated
him from the beast of self-will that enslaved the priest and Levite.
He was able to recognize himself in the wounded man because he
meekly accepted the lowly status conferred upon him by the
social and religious standards of his day. And in the recognition
born of shared woundedness, the Samaritan found strength to
take mercy on the wayfarer, extending to him the gift of love,
midwifing him back to physical health, and doubtlessly, inspiring
a spiritual rebirth similar to the one Adam nurtured in Henri
Nouwen. The Samaritan's weakness was his strength: the power
of enabling love. The priest and Levite's strength was weakness:
the blond beast's self-limitation of smugly arrogant disdain.

Jesus' story of the Good Samaritan clues us into two points
about the enabling power of love born from weakness, which we
would do well to keep in mind. Otherwise, we risk quick disillu-
sionment in our own efforts to practice merciful meekness. The
first is that even though the power of meek love is boundless, this
doesn't mean that the person who exercises it is some kind of tire-
lessly perfect superhero. Love, as Dostoevsky once said, can be a
harsh and dreadful thing. The sacrificial service it demands of us
can and at times will be burdensomely unwelcome. Even if the
spirit is willing, the weary flesh may balk. The supreme archetype
of loving-kindness, Jesus the Christ, sweated blood in
Gethsemane and pled for the cup of limitless sacrifice to be taken
from him. Nouwen tells us that gentle Adam occasionally
exploded in fits of inarticulate rage and frustration at the self-
emptying required of him. It's not too much to suspect that the
Good Samaritan may have been tempted to turn his head and

pass by the wounded wayfarer when he first spied him on the roadside, or that after he left him at the inn with the promise to return, he wished he could get out of his obligation.

We are, after all, but human, and it's only to be expected that our love for others at times will bring us heartsickness or a sense of resentful weariness. We may long to run away from those whose wounds call to us, to chuck the whole wretched business and flee to the hills. Even Jesus needed to get away from the crowds every so often (e.g., Matt 14:13; Luke 6:12). God himself, surely, must yearn to lay his burden down once in awhile and go on holiday.

So the strength of love doesn't mean that we'll never falter in our efforts to midwife others into being. We may as well admit this and prepare ourselves for it. But what it does mean—and this is the second point to remember—is that our *commitment* to loving-kindness remains steadfast, and that this commitment will see us through the rough times. Jesus *did* drain the cup of bitterness to the bottom, just as Adam persevered in his acceptance of who he was, and the Samaritan faithfully tended to the wounded man.

In the previous chapter we saw that the scriptural under-standing of divine *chesed* or *eleos* has it that God's loving-kindness remains steadfast through thick or thin. Those of us who have been reborn into our original oneness with God are likewise graced with the gift of steadfastness. And the basis of that resolve is the meek awareness that our essential connection with God and our fellows is the greatest of all blessings, that our dependency upon the mercy of God is an opportunity to live as fully as we can by showing mercy in return. Love may indeed be as Dostoevsky described it. But for the mercifully meek person who has sub-jected him- or herself to love in order to gain true freedom, its harshness and dreadfulness are but growing pains that herald the eventual blossoming forth into complete personhood.

The powerful weakness conferred by Christian freedom, then, once again underscores the inseparability of meekness and mercy. Mercy's awesome power to enable personhood must be built upon the vulnerability of meekness. Without both of them, the boundless capacity to love, which is the last and best expression of personal freedom, falls stillborn.

Enabling the Enabler

To be a person is to be free: free from the ensnarement of the beast, free to reconnect with God and one's fellow humans, free to lovingly midwife others into their own God-destined oneness. That freedom can only be attained through the spiritual gift of merciful meekness, a gift that extends ever wider to encircle all of reality in the unity of love.

This brings us to the final thing to be said about merciful meekness, and it's a fitting note on which to close this little book. The original connection between God and human beings is so intimate that our enabling of others into full being also mysteriously enables God to be fully God. God graciously midwives us into the new birth of personhood, and when we humbly receive the gift of life, we in turn become midwives for and of God. We who have been enabled now live in such a way as to enable the Enabler.

The fourteenth-century mystical theologian Meister Eckhart made this point in a startling commentary on the scriptural text that reads: "Behold, I stand at the door and knock; if any one hears my voice and opens the door, I will come in to him and eat with him, and he shall see me" (Rev 3:20). Reflecting on the verse, Eckhart says this:

> You need not look [for God] either here or there. He is no farther away than the door of the heart. He stands there, lingering, waiting for us to be ready and open the door and let him in. You need not call to him as if he were far away, for he waits more urgently than you for the door to be opened. You are a thousand times more necessary to him than he is to you.[21]

You're a thousand times more necessary to God than he is to you. This isn't our normal way of looking at things, is it? Even if we grant that Eckhart has indulged in literary hyperbole to make his point, the message is still unsettling. We typically think that the relation between ourselves and God is unilateral: we're utterly dependent on divine grace, yet God self-sufficiently stands alone with no need of our helping hand. Eckhart would certainly concur with the first claim, but asks us to reconsider the second.

Eckhart's assertion isn't as unorthodox as it might appear at first glance. The Hebrew Bible, after all, is the chronicle of a covenant between God and humans, and covenants by definition imply reciprocity of both privileges and obligations between the involved parties. In a business contract, the reciprocity is generally based on a mercenary quid pro quo: you do this, I do that, and we both profit. But in the Old Testament covenant between God and mortals, the exchange is one of mutually needed love: Yahweh promises to faithfully love the Hebrews into full being, and in return humbly asks that they help him to be what he is by loving him. The sacrifice for which God aches isn't a burnt offering, but loving-kindness—*chesed*. The mysterious implication is that God's well-being, if we may speak in such terms, is somehow dependent upon the human response to his covenantal overture.

The Christian Bible hints at the same point. In the Sermon on the Mount, Jesus tells his listeners that they're the salt of the earth and the light of the world (Matt 5:13, 14). Salt is in the business of preserving and enhancing what's good, the proper job of light is to reveal what's shadowed, and both aim at furthering God's plan for creation (Matt 5:16). Elsewhere, Jesus tells his disciples that he must lend a helping hand to the Father, and urges them to follow his example (Luke 2:49). Paul picks up this theme time and again, admonishing the early Christians to act in ways that not only please but serve God. In his famous image of the Body of Christ, Paul even goes so far as to imply that humans are the hands and feet, eyes and lips, of God (Rom 12:4–5). These and other texts gesture at Eckhart's claim: even as we need God, God needs us. The relationship is one of mutual, even if not equal, dependency.

We can make some sense of all this if we pause to consider the apostle John's claim that God is love. The essence of this love is the merciful enablement of being: God wills to love all reality into ripeness. This was the motive behind the original act of creation, just as it's the hope that keeps God faithfully lingering by the doors of our heart, and when that ripeness is achieved, God's eternal plan is accomplished. But God cannot force ripeness. Love that's crammed down the throat of the beloved chokes rather than enables. So God patiently—meekly—waits for us to recognize and gratefully receive his invitation to be. When we freely do so, we further the divine plan by enlisting as junior partners in the campaign to stretch the dominion of love. And when we take the God-gift of love to our brothers and sisters, we extend the circle ever wider. Even as we midwife their rebirths through merciful meekness, we help God come closer to his final goal of universal ripeness. In doing so, we progressively enable him to come into his own as the pure Love that grounds and sustains and receives love. God lovingly enabled us first, so that we might lovingly enable one another and, ultimately, him (cf. 1 John 4:19).

This, surely, is part of what Jesus meant when he said that our loving midwifery of the hungry, the thirsty, the forlorn, the sick, the naked, and the imprisoned is simultaneously an enabling act of love to God himself (Matt 25:35–45). More is at stake here than just our personal salvation. All of creation groans and travails for the final realization of God's plan (Rom 8:22). And so does God.

So let us enable God, and ourselves, and one another, as well as the stars and the seas and the earth with all its living things, by accepting the spiritual gift of merciful meekness. The promised freedom of full being—of *integritas*—doesn't belong to us alone. It is also the universe's, and it is God's, too. Blessed are the meek, blessed are the merciful. For in them, through them, and to them, comes the Kingdom.

Notes

Introduction

The chapter epigraph is from Thomas Merton, *Conjectures of a Guilty Bystander* (New York: Doubleday, 1989), 277.

1. Karl Rahner, *Foundations of Christian Faith*, trans. William V. Dych (New York: Crossroad, 1989), 403.

2. Anonymous, *The Cloud of Unknowing*, ed. William Johnston (New York: Doubleday, 1973), 127.

Chapter One

The chapter epigraph is from a sermon by Bernard, quoted in Jean Leclercq, "The Imitation of Christ and the Sacraments in the Teaching of St. Bernard," *Cistercian Studies Quarterly* 9 (1974): 36–54.

1. Friedrich Nietzsche, *The Will to Power*, trans. Walter Kaufmann (New York: Random House, 1967), 98, 117.

2. Friedrich Nietzsche, *Beyond Good and Evil*, trans. Walter Kaufmann (New York: Random House, 1966), 205.

3. Ibid.

4. Ibid., 204–5.

5. Ibid., 207.

6. Ibid.

7. Nietzsche, *The Will to Power*, 109.

8. Ibid., 129; *Beyond Good and Evil*, 74.

9. Friedrich Nietzsche, *On the Genealogy of Morals*, trans. Walter Kaufmann (New York: Random House, 1969), 45.

10. Nietzsche, *The Will to Power*, 118, 96.

11. Thomas Merton, *Entering the Silence*, ed. Jonathan Montaldo. *The Journals of Thomas Merton*, Volume 2 (San Francisco: Harper, 1997), 258.

12. Freud discusses the id in many of his works. But see especially *An Outline of Psychoanalysis*, trans. James Strachey (New York: W.W. Norton, 1949), chapter 1, and *New Introductory Lectures on Psychotherapy*, trans. James Strachey (New York: W.W. Norton, 1964), chapter XXXI.

13. Aristotle, *Nicomachean Ethics*, trans. David Ross (New York: Oxford University Press, 1986), IV.5, pp. 96–98.

14. Thomas Merton, *Turning Toward the World*, ed. Victor A. Kramer. *The Journals of Thomas Merton*, Volume 4 (San Francisco: Harper, 1996), 426.

15. André Louf, "Humility and Obedience in Monastic Tradition," *Cistercian Studies Quarterly* 18 (1983): 262.

16. *Mechthild of Magdeburg: The Flowing Light of the Godhead*, trans. Frank Tobin (New York: Paulist Press, 1998), 97.

17. Henri Nouwen, *The Road to Daybreak: A Spiritual Journey* (New York: Doubleday, 1988), 198.

18. Merton, *Turning Toward the World*, 205.

19. Henri Nouwen, *Adam: God's Beloved* (Maryknoll, NY: Orbis, 1997), 15, 30.

20. Ibid., 53.

21. Ibid., 49.

22. Ibid., 30.

Chapter Two

The chapter epigraph is from Jean Vanier, *From Brokenness to Community* (New York: Paulist Press, 1992), 51.

1. Friedrich Nietzsche, *Twilight of the Gods,* trans. R. J. Hollingdale (New York: Penguin, 1972), 118.

2. Ibid., 119, 118.

3. Ibid., 118.

4. Ibid.

5. Ibid.

6. Ibid., 199.

7. Friedrich Nietzsche, *The Gay Science,* trans. Walter Kaufmann (New York: Random House, 1974), 270.

8. Ibid.

9. Friedrich Nietzsche, *Ecce Homo,* trans. Walter Kaufmann (New York: Random House, 1969), 233.

10. Dietrich Bonhoeffer, *The Cost of Discipleship,* trans. Reginald H. Fuller (New York: Macmillan, 1963), 45–48.

11. One of the most popular modern champions of social selection is the novelist Ayn Rand. Both of her major novels, *Atlas Shrugged* and *The Fountainhead,* deplore those "meek" persons who hold back persons of strength and genius and thus retard social progress. The very fact that Rand's books are runaway best sellers suggests that many of us are quite sympathetic with her underlying Nietzscheanism.

12. J. B. Phillips, *New Testament Christianity* (New York: Macmillan, 1957), 68.

13. Thomas Merton, "The Good Samaritan," in *A Thomas Merton Reader*, ed. Thomas P. McDonnell (New York: Doubleday, 1996), 349.

14. Ibid., 350.

15. Martin Luther, "The Sermon on the Mount," in *Works*, Vol. 21, ed. Jaroslav Pelikan (St. Louis, MO: Concordia, 1956), 29.

16. Merton, "The Good Samaritan," 351.

17. William James, *Pragmatism* (New York: Longman, Green & Co., 1907), 88.

18. Robert Coles, *Dorothy Day: A Radical Devotion* (Reading, MA: Addison-Wesley, 1987), xviii.

19. Henri Nouwen, Donald P. McNeill, and Douglas A. Morrison, *Compassion: A Reflection on the Christian Life* (New York: Doubleday, 1983), 66–67.

20. Peter Maurin, *Easy Essays* (Chicago: Franciscan Herald Press, 1977), 9.

21. Helmut Thielicke, *Menschsein-Menschwerden* (Munich: R. Piper, 1976), 289–90.

Chapter Three

1. André Gide, *The Immoralist*, trans. Dorothy Bussy (New York: Random House, 1958), 9.

2. Ibid., 19.

3. Ibid., 50, 24, 25.

4. Ibid., 25–26.

5. Ibid., 55.

6. Ibid., 78, 80, 89. Part of this quotation is actually from a monologue by the character Ménalque, one of Michel's fellow

blond beasts. But since Michel tells us (90) that Ménalque's words perfectly express his own thoughts, I've taken the liberty here of combining them with Michel's.

7. Ibid., 90.

8. Ibid., 125.

9. Ibid., 129.

10. Ibid., 7.

11. Ibid., 145.

12. Ibid., 146.

13. Thomas Merton, *Dancing in the Water of Life,* ed. Robert E. Daggy. *The Journals of Thomas Merton,* Volume 5 (San Francisco: Harper, 1997), 48.

14. Martin Luther, *Christian Liberty,* trans. W. A. Lambert (Philadelphia: Fortress Press, 1957), 7.

15. Karl Rahner, *Foundations of Christian Faith,* trans. William V. Dych (New York: Crossroad, 1989), 402.

16. Jean Vanier, *From Brokenness to Community* (New York: Paulist Press, 1992), 21.

17. Ibid., 24.

18. Karl Rahner, "Freedom Regarded as a Dialogic Capacity of Love," in *A Rahner Reader,* ed. Gerald A. McCool (New York: Crossroad, 1984), 261.

19. Henri Nouwen, *Adam: God's Beloved* (Maryknoll, NY: Orbis, 1997), 30.

20. Ibid., 49.

21. *Meister Eckhart: A Modern Translation,* trans. Raymond Bernard Blakney (New York: Harper, 1941), 121–22.